SPYLESS IN TIRANA

An Albanian adventure

ALEX KLAUSHOFER

First published in 2024 by Hermes Books

ISBN 978-0-993323645

Hermes Books

www.alexklaushofer.com

'Everyone should come here. At least those who make use of the name *Europe*. It should be an initiation ceremony, because Albania is the unconscious of the continent. Yes, the European id, the fear that at night haunts slumbering Paris, London and Frankfurt am Main. Albania is the dark well into which those who believe everything has been settled once and for all should peer.' [1]

The origins of this book lie in what now seems like a distant time. In 2019, I set out to explore Europe by way of three of its lesser-known cities as part of research for a book. All were unknown to me: I arrived in each place for the first time, knowing no one. I had chosen them carefully, with each city illustrating an aspect of the trends and challenges facing Europe at that time. Cadiz, reputedly the continent's first city, represented Europe the old, a microcosm of Spain in its heyday but now in economic decline. Tallinn, capital of Baltic tiger Estonia and one of the world's most digitally advanced societies, exemplified

Europe the new. And the poorest of them all, the Albanian capital of Tirana, with its Muslim-majority population and desire to join the European Union, embodied Europe the aspiring.

The research for *A Tale of Three Cities* went well, and in early 2020 I was halfway through writing the first draft. Then Covid happened and, by the end of that year, I'd unexpectedly moved to Lisbon. For a while, I hoped to finish the book once things got 'back to normal', perhaps with the addition of the fourth city in which I was living. But gradually it became clear the world had changed to such an extent that the book I'd being planning about contemporary Europe was no longer possible. If I ever write about that time, it will be a kind of elegiac look back on a Europe-that-was wrapped up in a personal journey, perhaps something in the vein of Patrick Leigh Fermor's *A Time of Gifts* or Laurie Lee's *As I Walked Out One Midsummer Morning*.

But fast forward to 2023 and my time in Tirana, instead of receding into the back of my mind, became clearer and more vibrant. It was partly down to the nature of the place: Albania is a crazy country, both tragic and hilarious, and Tirana is possibly the most colourful city I've ever been to. But the other reason was that, after the experience of the Covid measures and with more centralised controls on the horizon, it was clear that the locus of a fifty-year dictatorship had lessons about freedom and human flour- ishing which we in the West would do well to heed. Under the domination of one man but with the cooperation and complicity of many, Albania 1944-1991 was a society built on the poles, each destructive in its own way of fear and political perfectionism. Fear isolated the country from the rest of the world, taking the form of a perennial enemy always ready to invade and conquer. Fear dominated the society internally: fear of the regime and fear of betrayal by others which could result in death or incarceration. Meanwhile, the direction in which Enver Hoxha took the country was driven by a monomaniacal vision of the perfect society, one that would take the scientific materialism of the age and the communist dream of complete equality to its highest expression.

The results of such experiments are well-known, but it seems that Western societies have forgotten that the patterns and behaviours which underlie them can easily return in new forms. In the twenty-first century, new dangers accompany the growing use of digital technology which could enhance surveillance and censorship beyond the Hoxha regime's wildest dreams. In our complacent liberal democracies, we do not seem to have grasped the psychology of authoritarianism and how the power-hungry manipulate human emotions to achieve their ends. We are too ready to dismiss new rules and restrictions as trivial or temporary, disregarding one of the biggest, most clearly-observable features of power: the controlling mindset, once it has a grip, keeps looking for new things to control. As Hannah Arendt pointed out in her seminal work on totalitarianism, this is a trajectory driven by a logic or, to put it in more contemporary language, an energy that only goes one way and ultimately ends in self-destruction.

Spyless in Tirana is nonetheless written as a travel narrative which reflects my experience at the time. I did not want to retro-fit responses that I did not have and have left it up to the reader to make whatever connections s/he sees fit. Readers wanting an updated view will find some explicit commentary on my Substack *Ways of Seeing*. As part of what was originally intended to be a full-length book, I present the Albanian material as a midform publication; what I like to call a 'travella' or short travelogue. You will not find the trendy tourist view of Tirana, home to much of the Albanian population which is still less than three million in this account. Instead, I've tried to tell the story of my experiences in the spring of 2019 in a human way and to give a glimpse into what was, from my way of seeing, almost another planet. In spite and because of its many problems, Tirana is testament to the diversity of humans and our endlessly creative, uncontrollable responses to life on earth.

Much of what you read in the following pages is thanks to the willingness of many people to share their time and knowledge with a foreigner. It follows that any mistakes or misunderstandings stem from my fallible Western eyes.

$$\text{❀} \quad I \quad \text{❀}$$

It was always going to be a strange trip. Albania had long fascinated me and yet I had very little sense of the place where I planned to spend a month. Having been shut off from the world for nearly fifty years, the little Mediterranean country was just starting to make its way into public consciousness in the West. By the time the communist regime ended in 1991, Albania was the third-poorest country in the world, its population subsisting on food rations. Private property and enterprise, car ownership and the keeping of livestock were all illegal.

Albania had long held a special place in my own consciousness as 'the country that got away'. Let me explain: in 1988, having inter-railed around Western Europe, I travelled to various countries in Eastern Europe by train, an informal inter rail trip which took in the German Democratic Republic, Poland, Czechoslovakia and Hungary. Somehow I'd persuaded a friend to accompany me on this bizarre adventure, one that – we didn't know at the time – presented the last chance to experience the strange world of the Eastern Bloc before it fell apart.

The trip had required the procuring of multiple visas, with entries and exits timed to the hour, and exchanging money to meet daily currency requirements, arrangements which, while complicated, had brought another Europe into my ken. But the People's Socialist Republic of Albania remained out of reach. While ruling the country according to Marxist-Leninist principles, dictator Enver Hoxha gradually discarded his allies, breaking ties first with Yugoslavia, then the USSR and finally China to pursue a unique isolationist form of communism. With its borders closed, the country was only accessible by invitation or if you joined a state-supervised tour.

One person I knew had done just that. Rob, a colleague in the charity where I worked after university, had gone on what he thought would be 'an enjoyably ironic holiday' with a mate, joining a group of Westerners who were closely watched by the secret police to make sure they didn't contaminate the local population with capitalist ideas. Arriving in Tirana just in time for the May Day Parade, the pair had found themselves amid crowds clapping their great leader. The towns were filled with statues of Stalin and almost every hill bore a slogan such as 'Long Live Enver Hoxha' spelt out in rocks. The pair spent most of their time visiting factories where their guides recounted statistics demonstrating how productivity levels fulfilled the country's five-year plan. At one point they opened their hotel room door to find a state official sleeping outside. Rob returned to work with an upbeat nationalist anthem which he would sing at dull moments in the office. Before long, I had learnt it well enough to join in:

. . .

For thirty years, the idea of Albania had lain dormant in my mind. Now, planning my own trip as part of research for a book, the song came back to me, a musical fragment that perfectly captured Hoxha's dream of self-sufficiency and his paranoia of the outside world. The Albania I would be visiting was very different, a country desperate to catch up with the West that aspired to join the European Union. And while it was struggling to meet the standards of a modern democracy, it was fast acquiring a reputation as an up-and-coming tourist destination, a hidden gem in south-eastern Europe offering mountain hikes and unspoilt beaches. Its capital, meanwhile, was presented as a hipster paradise full of trendy bars and cafes. Tirana had been transformed into a city of colour thanks to the ingenuity of its former mayor Edi Rama, an artist who had had the drab buildings painted in vibrant shades. It was a fairy tale-like story of a city made good.

Of course, Albania still had some negative images to overcome. Recently, the tourist board had launched a publicity drive aimed at persuading prospective visitors that the things Albania was well known for – drug smuggling, organised crime and human trafficking – were nothing to worry about. Entitled 'Taken by Albania', the campaign riffed on the 2008 film 'Taken' in which the daughter of the character played by Liam Neeson was kidnapped by Albanian sex traffickers. 'While we understand that perception might make for good movies, like "Taken", it's wholly untrue! In reality, Albania is a beautiful and incredibly safe place to visit and live,' gushed the copy. The reader was urged to sign a petition 'to get Mr. Neeson to Albania and Be Taken by its beautiful nature, hospitality and eternal traditions'.

I was excited about the prospect of discovering this singular corner of Europe. And while I knew no one in Tirana, I had an entrée into the culture. For the first couple of weeks, I would be working as a volunteer in the capital's first hostel. The hostel was in the centre and had been opened in 2005 by an Albanian-Dutch couple. From the description on Workaway, it looked ideal: such arrangements were supposed to facilitate cultural exchange and it looked as if the hostel was a model of the way Albania was opening up to the world, authentic yet internationalist. The listing pictured the owner, pony-tailed and relaxed, the globally-recognisable figure of the hippy. I made my writing project clear in my application and was accepted. For the second part of the trip, I booked an apartment to give me the privacy to focus on research and interviews. Apart from learning the word for 'thank you' – a multi-syllable workout for the tongue – I made no attempt to learn the language. As an independent branch of Indo-European languages with no close connection to any other extant tongue, Albanian was dauntingly difficult. No matter: I gathered that many, if not most, people in Tirana spoke English.

The taxi from the airport rushes through the darkness. My first time in Albania? Thank you. The driver's eyes crinkle ingratiatingly in the rear-view mirror. His English is limited and after a few more questions, the conversation peters out. I allow my gaze to settle on the blackness flowing past the window. Then somehow, without any change in the lighting, we have left the highway and are coursing through city streets. We must be in the outskirts of Tirana but there's so little light it's hard to get a sense of how close we are to the centre.

The driver turns into a side street and pulls up. 'Here,' he says. Peering out of the window, I remain seated. It is very dark outside. Can this possibly the centre of Tirana? 'Here, hostel,' repeats the driver. My eyes start to adjust and, staring into a pool of hazy light, I can just about make out the words TIRANA BACKPACKER HOSTEL painted in shaky capitals along a wall. I get out and cautiously accept my luggage from the boot of the car. Then I am alone in the middle of the pavement. In front of me are some metal gates and, beside them, an intercom. I press the button.

Moments later, the door is flung open by a bearded young man holding a guitar. I step through the gates and find myself in a courtyard. In front of me is the entrance of an elegant townhouse. A flight of marble steps leads up to some double doors which open onto a hall full of light. To my right is the kind of wooden construction you might find at a yoga centre, its curtained doorway revealing an interior of vintage and Indian furnishings. The space to my left is filled with plastic water tanks and bicycles. The young man has wheeled back into the shed leaving a large dog barking from the hallway of the house.

I stand clutching the handle of my suitcase. The dog has a face like a pit bull terrier but its large ears and mottled fur suggest a cross breed. Would a hostel have a dangerous dog? The velvety ears stand up in points and the head is tilted in concentration. The dog's gaze is fixed firmly on me. I hesitate and then, sensing that it's not so much barking at me as telling the humans about the new arrival, I mount the steps.

There is no one in the hall or in the side room which serves as reception. But soon a young woman bustles into the hall from the back of the house. She seems preoccupied as she gives me a hasty tour of the villa ending up in the first-floor dorm where I'll spend the night. 'Don't get too comfortable, you'll be moving,' she warns, patting the pile of mismatched bedlinen folded on the upper bunk bed. She leads me back downstairs and outside to a large patio at the rear of the building. A few people are standing, awkwardly, under the skeleton of a bar made of fresh pale wood. It had just been built in preparation for the new tourist season and congratulatory noises are being sent in the direction of its creator, a tall young man with dread-locks. A small, bearded man, his greying hair tied loosely back in a ponytail, is standing nearby. 'This is Ilir, the big boss,' says the young woman.

The man nods coolly in my direction. Under the harsh strip lighting of the new bar, he looks older and less care-free than the person in the photo. Dinner, I'm told, is being served inside; I should hurry if I want any. I join a group seated on cushions in a ground-floor room as a tray of beetroot fritters and bowls of salads are passed around. The meal is delicious but no one seems to want to talk, so afterwards I decide to go out and get my bearings in my new neighbourhood.

The darkness over Kavaja Street has a denseness that is almost palpable. As I walk down the road taking note of my new surroundings, the reasons become clear: there is not much street lighting and the low buildings leave a lot of sky. Some shops are still open and I pass several cafes, all with metal chairs and shiny plastic fixtures. The first has a large TV screen filled with a familiar figure. Edi Rama, former mayor of Tirana and now the Prime Minister of Albania, is extending his arm in a commanding kind of way. The next cafe also has a TV screen tuned to the same station, and so does the one after that: three cafes broadcasting the same recurring image of a commanding leader. Each one has a smattering of customers, all men with neatly-clipped dark hair who look strangely alike.

I walk on and am reassured by the presence of a few other women on the street. No one meets my eye as I pass. My apparent invisibility leaves me with a feeling of being neither safe nor unsafe, but oddly disconnected from my surroundings. I'm pleased to find a supermarket further down the road to buy the toiletries I couldn't put in my carry-on luggage. At the cash desk I realise I've already forgotten the word for 'thank you'. Scooping up my purchases, I mumble an inaudible sound and head back to the hostel.

In the dorm, a group of American missionaries is bedding down ahead of an early flight. There's a draft coming through the ill-fitting window and we agree that Tirana is much chillier than we expected at this time of year. Climbing into my bunk bed, I wonder if I've made a mistake. It's been a long, strange day since I started out at Gatwick. But, reminding myself I can get myself out of anything I don't like, I sink into sleep, surfacing briefly in the middle of the night as the missionaries gather their things and leave.

The crowing of a cock is followed by the call from a local mosque and a peal of church bells. Voices float up from the street below. I'm alone in the dorm. Sunlight fills the room.

I get down from my bunk, go over to the ill-fitting window and take a good look outside. In the street below, people are sitting outside a cafe, drinking their morning coffee in a leisurely fashion. The alienation of the previous night has gone and I feel the energy of life pulsating around me. Now I'm intensely curious about the strange new world I've landed in. Looking to the right, I see a concrete apartment block dominating the sky, its facade dotted with tatty awnings and grubby air conditioning units. Its windowless side bears the words 'Apartemente lluxsoze'.

I dress and go downstairs. In the light of morning, the patio garden at the back of the hostel has become an inviting space. A hotchpotch collection of sheds and verandas line its edges and small trees and clumps of shrubs provide oases of shelter for the little tables that are scattered about. Breakfast is spread out on the bar, a multicoloured feast of fruit, vegetables, eggs and toast. I eat mine with a Spanish couple who have been hitching around Albania and are delighted with everything, from the friendliness of the people to the health of the agriculture. Then I join the staff and volunteers assembling at the back of the patio; it seems I've arrived just in time for a collective workday.

The first task is to ready the garden and create an hospitable space where guests can eat and relax. The ground must be swept, the furniture cleaned and arranged in optimum positions. There's a lengthy group discussion about where the long table, which will host the communal meals, should go: here, or over there? Is it better this way, or that? Opinions and objections are freely expressed while Ilir hovers at the edge of the group, benign and a little detached. When the discussion finally burns itself out, he quietly authorises what has emerged as the decision. The next discussion concerns the fate of an old sofa, an asymmetrical construction upholstered in a brown floral fabric that dates it to the 1970s. The sofa is uncomfortable, says the volunteer who built the bar, but Ilir says he likes it.

'During the regime, almost everyone had something like this,' grins Edvin. As the friend who helped Ilir start the hostel, he is of an age to remember communism. 'It was one of only two or three models available.' I take a closer look. The sofa is of a sturdy construction and its asymmetrical appearance derives from inbuilt shelves at one end in which to store books, games or cigarettes. A consensus coalesces: the communist sofa will stay and become part of the seating for the main table.

Once the outside space is arranged and the little tables draped with cloths of different patterns and colours, the work party moves inside. I gather that the next job is to convert some of the downstairs rooms into dorms but no one explains anything or allocates tasks. In the room where I had dinner the previous night, I find Ilir erecting bunk beds and offer to help. I'm given the job of washing down the walls. 'They see everything,' he instructs. That done, I hold bits of bed while he bolts them together. We start to talk, sizing each other up like wary animals.

'You are writing one book,' he opens cautiously.

'Yes,' I agree.

'Will you write about the hostel?' His gaze remains firmly on the wooden frame he's constructing.

'Maybe. It depends if it's interesting.' In truth, I don't yet know.

'But in books things can be made up …' It's the beginning of an objection which I can't afford at this stage. I write non-fiction, I tell him firmly, so I only write the truth.

'Ah, but what it is truth?'

He seems pleased when I tell him I have a PhD in philosophy. Under Hoxha, he tells me, the ideological focus on the economic, industrial and scientific meant that everything except materialist philosophy was banned, even communist texts. Hegel, being an idealist, was completely out. And come to think of it, only some of Marx was okay, the parts that had been published in Stalinist Russia … What about Durkheim, I ask, with his attempt to bring a scientific approach to the study of society?

He doesn't know, and calls Edvin who studied philosophy in the last years of the regime and will have a better idea of what was allowed. Edvin tries to recall what books were available but struggles to come up with any names. 'In the end, we were just allowed to read what our leader wrote. Everything was, "This is right, that is wrong." Colours were not allowed.' He flashes an ironic grin and disappears.

Later, I do a training shift on reception. There seems to be a multiplicity of things to remember, with different categories of payment to record in colour-coded boxes on multiple spread-sheets in various word files. Oh, except when, and if … There are different views about when guests should pay but no written instructions to follow when no one else is beside me. There are emails to answer requiring a deeper knowledge of how things are done than I could possibly have, including an irritating message from a scouts' group requesting a discount on the already-cheap prices. Then the computer freezes and Ilir disappears.

The shift leaves me with a headache, so I take a walk in the dark to clear my head. This time I go further, to the far end of Kavaja Street. As I turn back, I notice that a man seems to be following me. To shake him off, I cross the road. He crosses behind me. I cross back and so does he. Eventually I give the man the slip by disappearing suddenly down a side street and making my way, fast, in the direction of the hostel via the back streets.

The next morning at the bar, Ilir's manner is conciliatory while mine is on the cool side.

'We will work together on reception,' he announces. 'You won't be alone any more. Look' – he points to the sky where a troupe of white doves is flying in formation – 'They often do that.'

I accept the apology. But it doesn't make sense, I tell him, to spend so much time training me given how little time I will spend on reception during my short stay. As I talk, I feel the vocabulary of Western corporate life creeping in: there's a risk of duplication and some things require institutional knowledge. But I don't have to talk for very long.

'Yes, you are right,' says Ilir. 'We will change the system.'

I'm astonished. Change the whole system on the suggestion of a newcomer? In my country, pointing out problems in organisations gets you ignored at best. Later, Ilir informs the others that, from now on, volunteer shifts will involve only the bar and cleaning, while the reception will be run by him and members of staff. 'Alex is right,' he says, spreading his hands. 'Learning all these things on reception is too difficult, on both sides.'

'It's nice that you listen,' I tell him, still mystified at this strange turn of events.

'Of course I listen,' he replies. 'You are here to help me. Advices are appreciated.'

'Do you know what management consultants are?'

Ilir shakes his head and looks at me wonderingly.

I tell him how big organisations hire intelligent professionals at great expense to analyse their problems but then ignore their recommendations and carry on as before.

'But everyone gets something,' says Ilir.

I hadn't thought of it like that. But if I dropped my idealistic conceptions, he was right: it was a process that provided the organisation with a sense of purpose and the management consultants with some money. Yes, everyone got something.

Over the next couple of days, I kept expecting to meet Ilir's wife. But gradually it emerged that she had returned to her native Holland with their three children, leaving Ilir to run the hostel alone. Except that he wasn't alone: Edvin still came and went from from the life he lived elsewhere and a couple of young employees did regular shifts. Two longterm volunteers effectively lived at the hostel: Kris who had built the bar and Fabi who cooked the evening meal. There were several more who stayed for a number of weeks or months during the tourist season. I had joined a team of both fixed and moving parts. I moved dorms twice as more rooms were opened for guests, reluctantly swopping a room that looked out onto the fruiting orange tree for quarters in the basement and began to drop into a new rhythm of life.

In the early mornings, the first sounds were of the chopping of vegetables. Breakfast was included in the price of a bunk, prepared by the person on the first shift. The first job was to boil the eggs; then came the chopping of the carrots, tomatoes, cucumber and white cheese. Was it me or were the colours of the food brighter than usual? Certainly the jam, locally-produced, was a world away from its mass-produced counterpart, a glorious, gloopy confection in which you could almost taste the sun in the fruit. Then it was a question of putting out the bread, piling apples and oranges into a bowl and making the tea and coffee. After that, as the trickle of guests turned into a stream and the patio was filled with morning chatter, it was a matter of replenishing the the dishes as people helped themselves. I liked seeing guests' faces on their first morning when, instead of the meagre fare that so often passed for 'breakfast included', they saw the length of the bar covered with fresh food.

Most of the food was bought in the surrounding streets. The market on the other side of Kavaja Street was crammed with stands displaying huge tomatoes, shiny aubergines and fresh strawberries. Women from the surrounding villages, aproned and head-scarved, ran ad hoc stalls composed of stacks of crates stuffed with herbs and greens they'd grown in their gardens. Delicatessens stocked locally-produced jam, cheese and olives. Every few yards, or so it seemed, there was a bakery selling byrek, parcels of filo pastry filled with spinach, cheese or meat. It was hard, amid all this sensory abundance, to remember that only a few decades before Tirana had been a grey place afflicted by food shortages.

Wandering the streets around the hostel, I tried to get under the skin of Tirana. It was not like any city I'd ever been to, while combining elements of many I'd known. It was too ramshackle and haphazard for a European city, nor did it resemble a Middle Eastern metropolis, with its endlessly-circulating people, noises and smells. A communist city? No, it had a vibrancy that lifted it out of the bleak uniformity I remembered from my trip around the Eastern Bloc. It was impossible to move with any speed, since I kept feeling the need to stop and try to make sense of what was in front of me. Things that didn't match were jumbled together: a tumble-down shack with a makeshift corrugated roof stood next to a new townhouse behind a smart wooden fence. There were concrete blocks ribbed with identical floors and dilapidated flats with exposed brickwork and hanging cables. The facades of buildings had windows and balconies of every conceivable shape and style: curvy and arched, straight and linear. The heights of buildings varied hugely, creating a skyline that was both jagged and random and the spacing between them was erratic. It was almost as if a giant child had turned a bag of toy buildings out onto the ground and got distracted before he could arrange them into some sort of order.

Ahead of me on the pavement, a hunched figure was propelling himself along with a crutch, dragging a useless leg behind him. A passer-by put a coin into his hand and I decided to give him something too. The face that turned to accept the coin was of someone with severe mental disabilities, and the sight of someone so vulnerable begging on the street sent a current of shock through me.

After all the visual dislocation, Skanderbeg Square was an oasis of calm. The granite flagstones which covered it merged into a lake of pearly coolness stretching over to a line of sleek, cream buildings that included the Opera House. A range of mauve-grey mountains undulated behind them. The limited palette and spaciousness of the place was unbroken by the people and bicycles moving across the square: here, I felt as if I was in The East.

But that was only the view looking directly to the north. Examined more closely, the square, too, was an amalgamation of the influences that had shaped modern Tirana. On one side was the National History Museum, a hulk of socialist realism with a large mural depicting Albanians from different times. On the other, the dome of the Great Mosque sat beside a minaret and nearby was the square shaft of the Clock Tower with its pointed Venetian roof. Beyond was the first of a row of Italianate buildings in brilliant red. In front of that, the national hero Skanderbeg sat astride his black horse in a horned helmet, his sword ready to defend his people.

Most perplexing of all was the tower-in-the making that hung over Skanderbeg Square. Its concrete sides were pocked with empty windows, giving the impression of watching eyes. Billboards around the square informed me of plans for more such towers. Another skyscraper, The Eyes of Tirana, a trendy construction of disjointed glass cubes, was envisaged. The billboards pictured the end result in hazy architectural blues accompanied by slogans which declared it would be 'IDEAL CONSTRUCTION' that was 'Beyond the realm of design'.

The day had a wintry feel and the few people outside were not lingering. Men hurried across the square and I noticed how uniformly clad they were, in short jackets of dark shades. The odd woman who clipped across wore the fitted garb of the office worker. It was almost always black and sometimes had a splash of red, perfectly echoing the Albanian flag. The people had a self-contained quality, a reserve that I couldn't put my finger on. Suddenly I felt very glad to have a temporary home in Tirana.

Sunday afternoon arrived, glowing with promise. My morning shift was done and it was a sunny day so I decided to venture further afield and take a proper walk around the south of the city. The past couple of days had proved that getting around Tirana, small as it was, could be perilous. The pavements had so many potholes and varying levels that it was easy to trip or turn your ankle unless you paid close attention to the ground underfoot. Obstacles and hazards appeared unexpectedly: a tree grew in the middle of a narrow pavement, a chasm opened up where steps led down into a basement shop.

Crossing the road was a major challenge. Under communism, the ownership of private vehicles had been banned and the few cars in the country were placed at the disposal of state officials. When the regime finally fell in 1991, Albanians made up for it. Huge numbers of cars were imported into the country and Mercedes Benz was a popular choice. A large shiny car quickly became a symbol of status, wealth, and freedom. But the sudden arrival of cars in a country where ordinary people had been expected to get around on foot, by bus or bike allowed no time for the development of driving skills or road safety. Tirana had pedestrian crossings, but cars only stopped at them with the greatest reluctance. When the green man showed and a crowd left the pavement, cars continued to edge their way across the red and white stripes, making as much progress as they could without running someone over. Elsewhere, cars paid no heed to pedestrians: crossing the road involved making a courageous decision to step out into the traffic, eyeballing the driver and hoping for the best.

It was hard to keep my attention on all the possible hazards. The previous morning I had stepped onto a particularly high kerbstone and found myself sliding down its shiny surface, falling … falling. Time slowed into an elongated moment, providing me with plenty of opportunity to reflect on the hardness of the ground and the injuries I could revive while alone in a foreign city. A passing man had put his arm out at just the right angle and broken my fall, pushing me back up into a upright position.

But on this spring day, I was feeling relaxed. I was starting to settle at the hostel and a new, interesting world lay before me, bathed in the golden light of late afternoon. I fetched the lead from reception and called the dog. Riza was always up for a walk, I'd been told. Half German shepherd, half pit pull terrier, she was an energetic cross breed. But she didn't get regular walks in the way a Western dog would: pets were a new thing in Albania. In fact, her life was altogether unconventional: like her owner, she was a vegetarian.

On the other side of the hostel gates, we shot down the street. Riza could not contain her excitement at being outside: every smell seemed to send her into a frenzy. Beyond each object was another requiring urgent investigation. At my end of the lead, I struggled to maintain a sensible pace. We sped past a middle-aged, leather-jacketed man who stared at me with delighted surprise; dimly I registered the fact that I must look like a foreigner. Finally, at the edge of a busy road, we came to a halt and I regained some control. Cars passed. Then, feeling my grip relax at a gap in the traffic, the dog pulled me off the kerb before I was ready, my ankle turned and I landed in a crumpled heap in the road.

Riza sniffed around the pavement, oblivious to what she had done. The pain in my ankle was excruciating; I could think of nothing else. Then some instinct told me to raise my head: a car was approaching from the distance. Terrified, I grasped the kerbstone and hauled myself closer to the pavement. The car passed, leaving me slumped half on the pavement, half on the road, breathing into the pain. Then a figure loomed above me. It was the leather-jacketed man who I'd passed earlier, holding out his hand. Helping me up, he escorted me to a chair outside a nearby cafe. 'Doctor?' he asked. I indicated that I would rest for a while, it would be all right. The man extended his hand, shook my own and departed.

For five minutes I rested outside the cafe, Riza uncharacteristically obedient at my feet. Then, obstinately reluctant to return to the hostel after so short a time, we set off again. Although the streets had a Sunday quietness, there was plenty to see. Two men were going through a dumpster and picking out things of interest; beside them a street dog was eating a meal of meat and bone off the pavement. We came to another major road. A man with an amputated leg was propelling himself fast along it with his hands, the empty leg of his jeans flapping as he went. Now that, I thought, was the way to move through traffic.

All the while, Riza pulled relentlessly on the lead, picking up unidentifiable things from the ground. From the crunching sounds that resulted, she was compensating for her vegetarian diet by chewing any bit of old bone she could find. The only other dogs on the street were strays, scruffy creatures with plastic tags in their ears and the sight of one triggered a volley of barking and extra tugging on the lead. Judging by people's reactions in the calm moments, walking a domestic dog was unusual: on seeing Riza, passers-by tended to give us a wide berth and one small boy screamed in fear. Matters were not helped by her desire to sniff strangers. Periodically I doubled up the lead, paused the walk and spoke to her sternly but the exercise only dampened her enthusiasm for a minute or two. By the time I reached the southern part of the city, I was starting to see myself the way others did, a woman with a limp being pulled along by a large dog which she could barely control.

'Sch@ztopk%*?' asked a woman pleasantly as I crossed a road rather faster than I meant. I was okay, I told her.

A quarter of an hour later and limping badly, I decided to head back to the hostel. But partly because of the difficulty of stopping to consult my map, I no longer knew where I was. The area we were in seemed somewhat rural, with houses and gardens strung out along a sandy track. And, with my physical strength ebbing, the struggle with Riza had become a battle of wills. She was as energetic as when we set out, if not more so, while I was now tired and disabled.

Finally, after winning a battle to stop Riza from pursuing something she'd glimpsed under a dumpster by a narrow margin, I admitted to myself that I was in need of help. A young man was standing outside a house and I asked him for directions. I was way off, he told me, in the suburb known as Youth Park. But he was walking to Rruga Kavajes and would show me the way. Would I like him to take the dog?

Gratefully, I relinquished the lead. Perhaps the problem, my new companion suggested, was my lack of Albanian: the dog would not understand commands in English. And with her resemblance to a pit bull terrier, people here would be frightened she might attack them. We introduced ourselves: Orgest was from the south of the country and had been working in Tirana as a software engineer for the past three years.

'Do you like it here?'

He waggled his head in equivocation. 'Somehow. I would prefer to stay in my town, but there's no work there. My town is quiet. We have a saying: "We need Tirana, but we don't love it".'

Tirana could be a good place to live, he went on, but it was badly run. The mayor was building towers instead of developing the public transport system and reducing the city's pollution. 'He's more interested in tall shiny buildings.'

He paused as he tried to get Riza under control. She was not behaving much better with her countryman, I noticed, but he was better equipped than I was to restrain her.

Like many people, Orgest was fed up with politicians. 'I am twenty-four, but I have never voted. I love politics and justice. When I was eighteen I wanted to study politics and law, but it was too difficult.'

'Would you join a movement?'

He shook his head. He had a lot of friends who worked in the public sector and had been invited to join a political organisation. If they did, they were then told what to do in their jobs – that was the path taken by the current mayor of Tirana. Many people still got their jobs through their political contacts. 'Three years ago, I got my qualification, applied for the job, and I got it. I prefer to do it like that.'

My companion's natural distaste for patronage and marked preference for a meritocratic system set him apart from the old political order. 'You're the first generation to be born free of communism,' I remarked.

'Yes, but my father and grandfather still have those ideas. Even if you're born after, you're kind of – he searches for the right word – 'infected by it.'

We had arrived at the gates of the hostel. I thanked him profusely and he handed me back the lead.

Grounded.

That night, my ankle had swollen to twice its usual size. By the next morning, it had swollen some more and I could barely put any weight on that foot. 'Easy day,' instructed Ilir, seeing me hobble to the bathroom. I could not do the planned cleaning shift and my usual method of getting to know a city, by walking its streets repeatedly, was out of the question.

I sat in the garden and tapped away on my laptop. But as the hours went by, I felt both bored and guilty. I hobbled across the garden, got myself up the steps into the building and limped along the passage to reception. Was there anything I could do that didn't involve much movement? Ilir looked up from the computer and said, with the faintest hint of exasperation: 'What can you do from the couch?'

I returned, dismissed and useless, to the garden. Plenty, was the response forming all-too-late in my head. I was a writer and this was the digital age. The English on the hostel website was far from perfect. Crossly, I buried myself in my research into Tirana.

Evenings at the hostel were becoming increasingly congenial. The first few nights had been chilly and, sitting in the garden, the household of guests and volunteers wrapped itself in blankets. But the temperature was rising and tourists were returning. The first guests of the season had been serious types: there was a Frenchman doing research into the gypsy communities of Albanian villages and a young Dutch woman doing a postgraduate thesis on religious pluralism. The new wave of guests were more conventional: young people travelling the world or European professionals taking a city break. Sitting amid a large group around the communal table, Ilir looked cheerful. The evening meal was proving popular: it cost only a couple of euros and was extraordinary quality for the price. Fabi was one of life's natural born cooks. She started thinking about what to cook the moment she woke up, she confessed, and spent the rest of the day shopping and preparing delicious vegetarian dishes for twenty or more.

With the new bar open, friends of Ilir's sometimes came by. The bar only served two drinks: beer and raki bought in the surrounding villages. After one small glass, I had found my drink. Albania's national tipple, made of twice-distilled grapes in a process that produced a liquid of white fire, was infused with whatever fruit, spice or herb that came to hand. The result was a spirit that was as powerful as it was delicious. Grape, plum, blackberry, ginger: the glass bottles containing the various flavours had their own shelf at the bar. Volunteers got a special deal: we were free to help ourselves to whatever drinks we wanted, recording them in a notebook to pay for them, at cost, later. Homemade raki was pure and it didn't take me long to work out that three good-sized measures over the course of an evening could get me mildly tipsy but leave no ill effects the next morning. A single glass one morning – it was a guest's birthday – just made my eyes sting.

One of Ilir's friends had lived in Britain for many years and spoke idiomatic English. Perched on a bar stool, he told me about a childhood under the last decade of the Hoxha regime. He had been twelve when communism ended. 'We didn't have any toys,' he said. 'We had to play with what was outside. The food was rationed, so you'd get a certain amount of butter per week, and mince or sausages, but not both. Bread, you could have as much as liked. Everyone had the same; no one had more than anyone else.'

He drew on his cigarette. 'It was a very poor country and that affected everything. You would get into trouble if you kicked a stone because that damaged the shoe, and there wasn't a way of getting another one.'

'Did you feel watched?'

'Yes,' he replied. 'We were trained by my parents to say the right thing: not to talk about not having enough food, for example, because under communism everyone was supposed to have enough. Spies were everywhere: they could even be your neighbours. People who did the wrong thing were sent off to live in cabins in the woods – we called them concentration camps – where there was nothing, just water and horrible food. A truck would come and they were told to load their things. Then a car would come for the people and the truck would go another way and they never saw their things again. It happened to my neighbours.'

His parents were Catholic and when religion was banned in 1967, religion became a private affair, another thing you didn't talk about. His parents missed the open expression of their faith. They told their children about Christianity, but forbade them from repeating anything outside the house. They'd named him Franz in an oblique tribute to St Francis, the saint on whose day he'd been born.

'Did you celebrate Christmas and Easter?'

'Yes,' he replied. His parents bought the presents much earlier to avoid attracting attention. 'And they didn't tell us it was Christmas, in case we said something to a friend, and he told his mother, and she told someone ... They told us it was something to celebrate before the New Year.'

'When the regime ended, were you happy?'

'Yes. Everyone was. My father took me to church straight away. Some people were very happy because they had got back something they had lost. For me, it was strange: "oh, you do the cross here" – he made the sign of the cross on his chest – 'and stand up there'. He laughed fondly at the memory of his belated introduction to religious ritual.

Twice a month, on the new and the full moon, Ilir lit a fire in an old metal drum and there was an informal party with music, its choice determined by whoever was on the bar. Ilir's friends would come and instigate rounds of raki drinking accompanied by a jaunty *gëzuar*, the Albanian for 'cheers'. Suddenly Ilir was at my side.

'What music did you like when you were young?'

Ah, such an easy yet important question. Like most of my generation, I had grown up effortlessly imbibing the pop around me, sampling different genres and tastes, ingesting, discerning and then moving on to a new musical phase. There was so much variety in the soundscape of my youth: soul, funk, Motown, reggae, ballads, disco and punk. But if I had to name one formative influence, I told him, it would be progressive rock and heavy metal. Ilir nodded. That was his favourite music, too. But for Albanians born in or before the 1970s, pop music came all at once, after the regime had fallen. In the 1990s they were assailed by a heady mix of current music and what had gone before, Phil Collins mingled with Marillion. 'And George Michael,' smiled Franz from his bar stool. From my first day in Tirana, I had noticed that in almost every establishment, whether cafe, supermarket or small shop, the air was filled with pop music. It seemed as if twenty-first century Albania couldn't get enough of the sounds of the West.

I was pleased to find Ilir in a receptive mood. Conversations with Albanians, I noticed, tended to end abruptly, as soon as the purpose of the interaction was concluded. It was a shame, because there was so much I wanted to know. Here was a chance to ask him about his memories of growing up under the Hoxha regime.

He recalled a carefree youth immersed in nature, with a lot of time spent in the village where his grandparents lived. The children would fight with wooden swords and thrash each other with nettles on an April holiday, for a reason he didn't remember but it had been great fun. His linguist father was one of the world's few experts in the Albanian language and had spent five years teaching in France, the only country with which Hoxha had retained normal relations. This had given Ilir the rare privilege of holidays in Paris: 'The best thing about it was the food – baguettes, bananas – things we never had under communism.' Going back and forth between the two countries, it was a good life. At that time, people were still well provided for and the public services were good, although very controlled. Even the two-week annual holiday was state-organised.

When Hoxha died in April 1985, Ilir went to school as usual. But no one in his class knew how to react: should they be happy or sad? Then the teacher took the lead, enacting a faux 'boo hoo' – Ilir mimed putting his knuckles over his eyes – and the children followed suit. Ramiz Alia, president since 1982, took Hoxha's place. The stifled country was well and truly in decline and by 1991, the food shortages had got so bad that you had to queue for bread, with men and women forming separate lines. As the regime started to crumble, opinions were divided between those who were for change and those who weren't. When the communist government finally collapsed, there was a great sense of freedom. People came out into the street to listen to music. Albanians were going out at night for the first time.

I was puzzled. 'Why didn't they go out before? Because nightlife is capitalism?"

'Yes,' he replied. 'Because nightlife is capitalism.'

Did he or Franz remember 'The Pick and Gun'? The two men looked blank, so I sung the verse I knew. Almost immediately, Ilir picked it up, followed by his friend; together they sung a few hesitant lines. The tune was melodic but unexceptional and stayed in a safe middle range. I begged for more – please, I've waited thirty years – and they went again, this time singing several verses with growing confidence.

'We almost have the whole thing,' said Ilir. 'We will sing it to you tomorrow.'

                                ❦   3   ❦

By way of compensating for my sick leave, I had
persuaded Ilir to let me improve the English on the hostel
website. He seemed pleased at the idea but didn't like the
process of discussing the changes, wriggling and pulling
faces like a recalcitrant child. 'Ah, this English,' he sighed
when I told him that describing a founder of the hostel as
'missing' sounded rather alarming. The exercise high-
lighted the absence of a standard of correctness in
Albanian and helped to explain some of the unfortunate
phrases I had seen on the streets of Tirana: a cafe called
'My Last Supper' and a travel agency with 'Be Taken by
Albania' above the door.

While I was enjoying my shifts at the bar, the cleaning
shifts were proving surprisingly complicated. Everyone
seemed to have different ideas about what was involved,
the most specific instruction being to make the outside
space 'look nice for everyone'. It was clear that the
showers and dorms had to be thoroughly cleaned, but
only two cleaning products were available: 'Spic Span' for
the floor and 'Smack Disinfectant' for everything else. I

was puzzled: judging from the vast selection in the local supermarkets, Albanians adored cleaning products. After a couple of shifts I became so frustrated about cleaning the toilets that I decided to clarify matters. I went to reception.

'Can I talk to you about cleaning products?'

Ilir looked up from the computer and gave me his full attention.

I sat down and gave a brief talk about the difference between toilet cleaner, limescale remover and bleach. I was surprised at my fluency on the subject: I loathed plastic packaging and was decidedly minimalist in my own domestic arrangements. But Ilir was staring at me. On his face was what I was privately starting to call 'The Albanian look', a wide-eyed gaze with an almost awe-struck quality. Exactly what it meant was hard to fathom.

Taking some money from the petty cash drawer, he got up. We would go, immediately, to the nearby Spa and buy some toilet-specific products. He still had The Look as we walked down the road. 'You're looking at me like I'm mad,' I probed. 'No, it's not that,' he replied but did not elaborate.

In the aisle which stocked the toilet products, a bewildering array of plastic bottles was spread out along the shelves. I summoned Ilir, who had headed straight for the laundry section, and we surveyed the scene: rows of WC Net, Duck, Domestos in bottles of blue, green, yellow and pink, each colour denoting the addition of extra substances or a particular scent. There was a large selection of plastic dispensers that you could lodge in the toilet bowl to dispense a continuous supply of product. Although I personally disapproved of such items, in my current role as cleaning coach, I felt duty-bound to explain their purpose. That done, I moved on to the next issue.

'Do you' – I hesitated, feeling laughter rise in anticipation of how the question would sound – 'do you have a problem with limescale?'

Briefly, we doubled up in the aisle. Then, regaining sobriety, Ilir started to pick up various bottles, asking my opinion about each one. 'Read the labels,' I told him. Left to his own devices, he would buy exactly what I suggested. But I felt strongly that, as hostel boss, he should make his own, informed decisions. Finally, he made two judicious choices and we started to move in the direction of the till. Still Ilir hesitated.

'Should we get the plastic thing?' he asked uncertainly.

My foot largely healed, I resumed my exploration of Tirana. After my hyper-local introduction to the city, I was gaining a belated understanding of its layout. From Skanderbeg Square in the north the elegant Dëshmorët e Kombit Boulevard ran like a spine to Mother Teresa Square in the south. Nearby was the sports stadium and a bit further on, the Artificial Lake served as the city's main green space. It was well used by people of all ages: parents patrolled with their children, young people worked out on the exercise bars and old men sat playing dominos among the trees.

Tirana was small and its landmarks memorable. The River Lana, a mountain stream that ran through a concrete channel fringed by trees, marked the half-way point between the north and south poles of the city centre.

Nearby stood the Pyramid, completed in 1988 as a museum of Hoxha's legacy but never used. The concrete structure was half-derelict, its walls covered in graffiti and its windows broken. It was used by the local youth as a climbing frame, and teenager boys could often be seen scaling its sloping sides.

Nearby was Kometiti, a cafe-museum furnished with memorabilia from Albania's recent history, especially the communist era. There were vintage television sets from my early childhood and transistor radios from before my time. Sitting on the toilet, I was surprised to see a shelf of Hoxha's books beside me. The dictator had been a prolific writer and produced thirteen volumes of memoirs, amounting to some seven thousand pages. Flavoured raki was the house speciality: behind the bar beamed glass bottles containing almost any flavour you could think of, from cinnamon to chilli.

One rainy day I went to the National History Museum in Skanderbeq Square. The socialist realist mural over the entrance told the history of the country's struggle for identity in a picture. To the left, a group defended the country against Romans and Ottomans with spears and shields, to the right some early twentieth century figures were using guns against the Italians and Germans. Forefront and centre were three figures marching determinedly into the glorious communist future: a woman holding aloft a rifle, a worker with his sleeves rolled up and a becapped man bearing a large Albanian flag which unfurled behind him. What energy! What vigour! 'The Albanians' told a story of defiance, national pride and triumph viewed through the lens of the early 1980s.

Inside the lobby, two young men in national folk custom were sitting on a sofa, engrossed in their mobiles. They were joined by two young women, one wearing a braided dress of black and red, the other decked in clouds of white and gold. 'Are you hired by the museum?' I asked them. 'The municipality, to promote the traditional costume,' replied a young man in a brocade waistcoat. Usually they stood outside, he went on, encouraging visitors to come in. 'But it's raining …' The group eyes slid ruefully towards the grey world beyond the doors.

The museum was organised into 'pavillions' covering different periods of Albanian history. A cabinet in the first pavillion displayed some of the first traces of human life in the area: flint stones dating from the Middle Palaeolithic period. In the Neolithic Age, squat male figures held sticks in front of a model cave. Next came pots and axe heads from the Copper Age. The displays were accompanied by lengthy commentaries in Albanian and English: 'The basic feature of the Copper Age is the emergence of copper metallurgy which gave the name of the epoch,' the sign informed me. 'Extracting and processing of this new metal were complex processes. The man taken care to such activities, gaining economic power, a fact that has to do with the beginning of patriarchal gender.'

Indeed. I moved rapidly through the following sections and continued to the upper floors of the museum. The place was virtually empty. Somewhere between prehistory and the twentieth century, the English petered out and, by the time I got to the Communist Terror pavilion, there was very little explanation.

I stood in front of a display labelled 'Rezistenca Anti Komuniste 1945-1948', puzzling over its contents. The main item was a beige waistcoat that would fit a large child. 'The doublet of Nazif Raska. Executed in 1945,' read the label. Next to it was something that looked like a stone but was in fact a 'piece of bread preserved by the family of Elez Kaloshi killed by the forces of the prosecution while eating this bread in 1945.'

A curator emerged from a shadowy corner. There was, she indicated, a lack of interest in labelling the Communist era; she would try to explain the displays to me but was sorry about her English. I could already hear that it lacked grammatical structure and was peppered with words of Italian and Albanian, but it had a vividness that communicated well. With no other tourists in sight, she had clearly decided to become my personal guide.

She led me to a black pillar in the middle of the room. A long list of names scrolled down it, with numbers beside them. These, she explained, were the names of political prisoners and the years they spent in prison. I understood that '*Sani Dangellia 43 vjet*' had died in prison at the age of forty-three. We moved onto a display of black and white photos entitled 'Shqiperia Burg': low buildings of concentration camps and grim interiors accompanied by sketches of crammed bodies. A nearby glass case contained objects of prison life: some traditional Albanian socks, a pair of glasses and a set of bright green dominoes. Next to them was the remains of a grimy garment patched out of things of different textures. One trouser leg remained intact while the other was in the process of disintegrating. The trousers had belonged to Gjon Vatnikoj Tunxhij, and had been mended by his mother Mrika with her own hair, explained the curator. Examining the hairy tangle, I felt slightly sick.

We moved on to another photo display. The thirty-five portraits showed women of all ages who had all been prisoners of concentration camps. I recognised the face of Musine Kokalari, Albania's best-known female writer and an early critic of the regime. Arrested in 1946 at the age of twenty-nine for campaigning for multi-party elections, she spoke defiantly at her trial: 'I do not need to be a communist to love my country. I love my country even though I'm not one. I long to see it make progress. It is true that you won the war, you won the elections, but that is no licence to persecute people whose political opinions are different from yours. You are punishing me for my ideas. I won't ask for pardon because I have not done anything wrong!' Kokalari spent sixteen years in prison and a further period doing hard labour before dying of cancer in 1983. It was hard to fathom that the nice-looking young woman in the picture had led such a life.

'Were any of your family imprisoned?' I asked my guide. She was in her fifties and would have grown up under Hoxha.

'No – familia have attenzione. Close mouth – see a lot – no speak.'

'Are things better now?'

'Now – speak, but money is a very big problem. Before, in perioda communista, we go on holiday, to the beach. Now I no go to the beach. Son, a cook in a restaurant in Blloku, but earns very little. The politika is very bad – corruption and droga. Tirana, it's very contraste. You see modern building and primitive house. You see a Mercedes car and a dog in the street.'

'Come'. She led me into a corner behind a pillar. Behind a glass door was a reconstruction of a small, dimly-lit cell. On the floor was a tin plate and a mug along with an upended helmet which apparently served as a toilet. 'Here, eighteen persons. Fifty degrees in summer, minus five in winter.' Blood dripped down the back wall, ending in some shaky letters. It came, explained my guide, from someone who cut himself in order to write his last protest two hours before being executed: 'It says: "Viva Albania. No like communism".'

A good portion of the nearby wall was covered with images of Hoxha. He was a handsome man, with the fleshy, regular features popular in mid-century Hollywood. In one shot he embraced Beqir Balluku, an ally he subsequently had executed; in another he was with Prime Minister Mehmet Shehu, who died in disputed circumstances. Other pictures showed him in meeting rooms, doing the important work of running The Republic and standing in a row of men, all making the same clenched salute.

'They say very beautiful – the Number One visage in Europa,' said my guide. 'But double standard – another it's a killer. It's very contraste – visage and heart. When greeting people he threw flowers, it's very romantic. You know the 1st May? It's parada.'

Enver Hoxha was the son of a Muslim cloth merchant in southern Albania and had, by all accounts, a normal childhood. As a young man he studied in France and Belgium but, on returning home, displayed no particular interests or ambitions. He taught for a while in his old school and then, with family help, ran a tobacco shop in Tirana. The turning point of his career came in 1941 with the foundation of the Communist Party of Albania, later called the Party of Labour. He became leader, his biographer Fevziu suggests, largely because his lack of political activity kept him out of power struggles and made him the least threatening candidate. He was good-looking and spoke well.

In 1944, Hoxha became Prime Minister of Albania, beginning a rule which was to last for the next forty-one years. He set about developing the country according to a vision that combined communism with nationalism. There was a strong focus on industrialisation and on achieving self-sufficiency through collective agriculture. Electricity was brought to every district and public services were extended to the most rural areas, giving everyone access to health services and education. Illiteracy was virtually eliminated in a population that, at the start of his leadership, could barely read and write.

It was a leadership characterised by brutal repression. Hoxha built prisons and camps to accommodate those who posed any kind of threat to his regime. In a population that was only about a million and a quarter in 1945, tens of thousands of people were imprisoned, with many thousands more executed. Among those close to him, purges and killings characterised his rule from the outset, extending to his brother-in-law and his best friend from his schooldays. By 1982, Hoxha had eliminated every man who had been his interior minister, a record almost equal to Stalin's. Those whose cards were marked would know nothing of their impending fate: Hoxha would be friendly to their faces and soon afterwards order their execution.

In the National Gallery I got a clearer idea of how Hoxha wanted to be seen by the public. The art gallery had an extensive collection of socialist realism, depicting life to a formula prescribed by the regime. As a would-be teenage art buff, I had loved socialist realism from the USSR. There was something so cheerful and childlike about it, with its bright colours and industrious scenes. The Albanian paintings in front of me were similar, but their subjects had an added vigour that was pleasing to the eye. Muscular men and strong-looking women strode about wielding heavy tools, clothed in serviceable fabrics and sporting bright kerchiefs. A group of men continued to operate heavy machinery in the face of a storm; a particularly sturdy woman carried a pickaxe on her shoulder, eyeing the viewer with a steady gaze. And it wasn't all work: in a picture reminiscent of the Janet and John books of my childhood, a family of four walked through the mountains, their enjoyment of the fresh Albanian air evident in their glowing complexions and cheerful expressions. Another picture showed children crouching in a playground, clustered around a chalk drawing of a rifle.

A young woman was hovering nearby, smiling gently. 'These were painted in communist times,' she explained. 'The artists couldn't paint what they wanted. You see the people are smiling: they are happy, but not really.' I wanted to know the names of the artists but the labels were being redone and hadn't been put back up yet. 'Sorry,' she smiled.

One large painting showed Hoxha standing outside the Academy of Arts in a greatcoat, the picture of reassuring masculinity. He was surrounded by an adoring public, some with their faces turned towards their leader while others – the artist had to solve the dramatic problem of turning one's back to the audience – looked to each other to share their joy. A head-scarved woman was spreading her hands in a declamatory way – Ta-Ta! – and a small boy was clapping. I stared at the picture, fascinated. The scene it depicted called something specific to mind, but I struggled to think what it was. Then it came - the picture resembled the congratulatory, whole-cast scene at the end of a musical. But with one difference: the entire focus, and all the congratulation, was on one man.

'He was quite good looking,' I remarked.

'Yes,' smiled the young curator.

And then somehow we were both laughing as we stood surveying the picture. I wasn't sure why the attendant was amused, but I knew why I was. It bubbled out of the happy recognition that things change, that thirty years after I hadn't been able to visit this cloistered country, here I was, laughing with a new generation about the absurdity of trying to mould reality according to the will of a single man.

Although I'd been in the gallery little more than half an hour, it was time to leave. Checking the opening hours online before, I'd found two different closing times – seven and eight o'clock. But on arriving at the gallery, the woman in the ticket office told me the actual closing time was six o'clock. Handing over the money, I expressed something between confusion and a complaint. 'Everyone says that,' smiled the woman. 'Every day of the week.'

With the curators hovering anxiously nearby, I sped along the gallery, taking photos so that I could at least study some of the artworks later. I already knew which was my favourite. It pictured two well-built young men balanced on a pylon high above the mountains, a brilliant blue sky blazing behind them. The workmen's demeanour betrayed nothing of the vertiginous height at which they were perched, nor did their relaxed pose suggest they'd been doing anything more onerous than lifting kittens. The mens' eyes gazed confidently into the distance. It was a little how I felt on a plane, cruising above the clouds towards some happy adventure.

The next day, I showed the picture to Edvin.

'Too Western. Too futuristic,' he said, peering at the computer screen. The picture reflected one phase of the way the Hoxha regime demanded art should be done, he explained, in this case a utopian vision of the fully industrialised society. 'There were waves when it was more liberal, and then it got strict again. Someone would come and say, "That looks funny", and suddenly it was wrong. You never knew what the rules were.' One artist had got into trouble for painting an old man sitting by the fire. 'They said it was too dark, not happy enough. I think the artist had a bad ending.'

His grandfather, he went on, had been the mayor of Shkoder, the northern city reputed for its jokes against communism. He was suddenly removed from office for no reason. When asked later about the reason for his fall from grace, his grandfather said: 'You know, I thought about that. I think it was because they had taken everyone else in Shkoder, and I was the only one left.'

$$\text{❧} \quad 4 \quad \text{❧}$$

I was sitting on the blanket box that contained the dirty bed linen in the hall when Ilir went past and gave me a puzzled look. 'I need to be near the router,' I explained. 'The internet connection's bad and I'm trying to get my head around judicial reform. I've got a meeting later.'

It was proving easy to set up meetings with key people. Albania was unlike Spain, where emails and calls tended to be ignored, but like Lebanon, where everyone wanted to meet a visiting Westerner. Tirana was a small place; people were generous with their time and eager to communicate with foreigners.

'Oh, you should talk to Edvin – he's a journalist,' said Ilir casually. 'He's the news anchor for News 24.'

I stared at him in surprise. Edvin, who helped to run the hostel and could sometimes be found cleaning the toilets, was one of Albania's main newscasters? 'Why didn't you tell me?' I asked reproachfully.

Ilir shrugged. 'I don't know.' He really didn't; he was the archetypal hippy, the opposite of the Albanian men I saw on the streets. He went about barefoot and preferred not to have too much on his mind. His business partner and old friend Edvin was a completely different personality: interested in politics and quick-minded, the kind of person I'd sometimes met who inexplicably transcended the limits of their background. Of course he was a leading light in this little country. Ilir was clearly thinking along similar lines, for he said admiringly: 'he remembers everything.'

I got off the blanket box and found Edvin on the reception desk. 'Can I talk to you about judicial reform?' I asked.

'No,' said Ilir, who had followed me. 'He's working here.'

'Five minutes,' I argued.

Edvin and I went to out to the front steps so that he could smoke while we talked. Albania's system of justice was currently being overhauled so that, as befitted a democracy, the law could be applied to everyone equally. In 2016, under pressure from the European Union and United States, the Albanian parliament had approved a reform package which included establishing a vetting process so that judicial appointments would not be made on the basis of money or connections. Prospective judges and prosecutors were henceforth examined to ensure that the assets they'd accumulated during their careers had been acquired legitimately, their record scrutinised for professional misconduct and possible ties to organised crime. The process was overseen by experts from the EU and US, but progress was slow. Only a small proportion of the judiciary had successfully passed the vetting process, with many sacked and others resigning ahead of evaluation. Meanwhile, there was a huge backlog in the courts and, with legal cases mounting, public trust in the system was falling rapidly.

There was no doubt that judicial reform was entirely necessary and that the challenge of achieving it enormous. But Edvin was unconvinced about the importance of meeting the requirements of the EU: in his opinion it would be far more worthwhile for Albania to develop connections with countries such as France, Germany and Britain. 'Many people here think were still in the nineties,' he said. 'Sincerely, I don't care what the EU decides. It's not in a position to put any pressure – it doesn't know what it will be itself in the next few years.'

That afternoon, an urbane looking man with floppy grey hair hurried towards me, hand outstretched. I was relieved that Neritan had come down from his office to meet me. It was on the other side of Mother Teresa Square, a big open space over which cars roamed freely. He had told me to call him on reaching the square and, as I stood surveying the traffic, I realised I hadn't a clue how to get across without getting run over.

Neritan Sejamini was the editor of EXIT, an independent English-language news website about the Balkans founded in 2015. He had been introduced to me by Alice Taylor, a British woman who had arrived in Albania some eighteen months earlier and taken the country by storm. She had established a successful blog called The Balkanista, wrote for Exit, engaged in frequent polemics with the political establishment and was expecting a child by her Albanian boyfriend. Neritan was clearly something of a powerhouse himself: navigating an apparently effortless path through the traffic, he was already in fluent flow about where Albania was on its journey towards democracy. 'After the hope of the 1990s, we are in a new phase of control,' he said. 'Things go in cycles and change takes time. You won't see much in the lifetime of a person; it takes hundreds of years.'

On the other side of the square, Neritan led me up a side street and into the modern block of flats where EXIT had its editorial quarters. With its tiled floors and neutral colours, the apartment didn't make a bad office. Several people nodded in a friendly way from behind their desks as we made our way to the meeting room. After we'd installed ourselves at the table, he picked up the thread of the conversation. Judicial reform was central to tackling the corruption that had been endemic in Albania for so long and meant that, for those with the right connections, wrongdoing was never punished.

'Total impunity – we don't have anyone ever brought before justice for corruption. This is a huge problem,' he said. Far from diminishing after communism, the reach of corruption had extended, spreading from petty deals to the political order itself. 'STATE CAPTURE!' His voice rose to a crescendo as he described the current situation, one in which even the laws that governed the state were influenced by private interests. That fact affected all aspects of Albanian society, employment and media, as well as its public institutions.

'This has been going on for many, many years,' he went on. 'There have been people who were genuinely interested to change it but the problem is that they don't know how to start. It's like a vicious circle. And suddenly they realise that the society is going to become a failed state and they come up with an idea which is more like something from the movies than reality.'

'Who are "they"?' I asked.

'The international community,' Neritan replied. 'Also Albanian intellectuals, people that genuinely want to change things but are *so* tired, having tried everything, with everything failing, that they have come to blame the Albanians as a people that cannot make progress. But they are still trying because Albania is there. It wants to be part of the EU, so you cannot ignore that.'

He paused. 'You ought to know that in Albania, the foreign powers have a tremendous influence. An American ambassador is one of the most powerful people in the country. Everything he says will be discussed, everywhere; people will try for weeks to find out "what did he mean by this?" It's the same for the EU ambassador.'

Albanian politicians took foreigners' views into account when policymaking as they didn't want to be condemned by the wider world. 'They always are very careful of what the foreigners say. Because when it comes to Albanian people, they believe that the Americans, British, Germans, French or Italians think all the time about Albania, love Albania, want the best for Albania, and they will sacrifice everything for Albania. This is stupid, this is naïve, but that's how it is.'

I couldn't conceal my astonishment. In Britain, I didn't know anyone who ever mentioned Albania. 'Where does that come from?'

'From communism,' replied Neritan. He skated rapidly over the history of the country prior to the dictatorship, from the Ottoman rule to King Zog's alliance with Italy. 'So we have lived under someone big all the time. And then, during communism, we flirted with Yugoslavia, then

Russia, then China. We always had a big brother who would take care of us.'

'Like a kind of parent.'

'Yeah,' he agreed. 'And then we have our leader, our great leader, one of the greatest men in the history of mankind, whose ideas will light the world for eternity ...' His voice rose dramatically to express the godlike status Hoxha had held. 'When the regime collapsed, almost everyone in Albania had been brought up under communism: there was no outside influence whatsoever, it was like North Korea. We were produced as human beings, completely manipulated. In 1991, the average age was twenty-something, which meant that entire generations didn't know anything else but socialist Albania, our great leader and his teachings.

'This idealisation of the Western world started during the last years of communism when the economic crisis was severe and everything was rationed. During the summer, we could sometimes get Italian TV and saw a glorious world, shining with advertising. And then foreigners came and helped us with everything, When The Transition started, it brought us a lot of aid, from humanitarian aid to technical assistance – we didn't know anything. Half of Albania migrated, mostly to the West. So we have a kind of idealisation of the West. We don't have much experience of self-governing, and we don't trust our own government.'

Everything he said made sense. It explained a lot about my experience in the hostel, how Ilir, in the absence of his Western wife, looked to foreign volunteers for ideas and support. It explained The Albanian Look and why he believed me implicitly when I talked about cleaning products. Alice had shared similar experiences in her adopted homeland with me: 'Being a foreign woman here – there are immense double standards between how I am treated and how an Albania woman would be treated,' she'd said. 'They put foreigners on a pedestal: we're more likely to be believed, we're more likely to be trusted. I could tell a certain Albanian person the sky is green and they would believe me. But if an Albanian said it, they would say they're an idiot.'

Meanwhile, Neritan continued, the foreigners trying to reform Albania's justice system were applying the same formula they'd used unsuccessfully in other countries. Domestically the whole enterprise had got sucked into political games, with the government ostensibly embracing the anti-corruption agenda and the Opposition portrayed as anti-reform. The foreigners were manoeuvred into defending the government: 'Rama framed it as "they are against justice reform, I want it clean, and they don't"'. Meanwhile the country was left without a functioning justice system to enforce the rule of law.

Neritan's words recalled the complex troubles of the Middle East with problems so deep-rooted, the connections between the various actors so opaque that attempts by outsiders to intervene, however clever or well-meaning, didn't have a chance.

'What would it take to bring change?'

'Information, education,' he responded immediately. 'Without political literacy, without informed citizens, you cannot have democracy. Albanians are still waiting for the government to solve every problem, even problems which are community-based. They don't understand that unless you distrust government, you are vigilant, it will become a monster.'

He had started Exit as a blog with a Dutch and an Italian as a modest way of fostering political literacy. The publication had no funding and few of the people who worked on it received any payment. Donations and the odd commercial project helped towards the running costs. He remained passionately committed to editorial independence.

'One thing that is sure,' he concluded. 'If you get money from politics, you are dead. If you get money from business, you are dead.'

His phone rang and our time was up. One of his colleagues took me downstairs. In the patch of land beside the apartment block, bulldozers were ploughing up the mud. 'A few weeks ago, it was all green,' said my guide ruefully.

Alba Cela smiled when I told her about my falling in Tirana. 'This is a chaotic country; you have to get used to it. In time, your body will adapt.' She added: 'I lived abroad for six years. When I came back, I was scared to cross the road.'

We were in the cafe on the ground floor of the Albanian Institute for International Studies. It was a chic, pleasant space furnished in light wood and cream, a world away from most of Tirana and smarter than many places in London. As executive director of the think-tank, Alba was well-placed to add to my understanding of Albania and the identification of its people with the Western world.

Like many people I spoke to, she referred to the current period as The Transition, a phrase which acknowledged where the country had come from and where it hoped, quite soon, to get as it moved from an impoverished communist regime to a Western democracy.

'In the first years, it was very difficult to discover the world and get the pace of what had happened in the world,' she explained. 'It was a very difficult transition on all fronts, not just political and economic, but for each and every individual. All the values changed, the values that guide you in your life. How many coped with this is that they left, so we had huge migration to Greece, Italy and other countries. What we see now is people leaving because of a lack of hope and high levels of corruption.'

Amongst the remaining population, great hopes were placed on the EU; all the surveys indicated a strong preference for joining. 'The lowest there's ever been is eighty-two per cent in favour of EU; the highest is ninety-seven per cent. We were an isolated, communist, poor country and the destination is Europe. So this whole process of joining the EU is not bureaucratic for us; it means the end of The Transition and the start of a new chapter for Albania, an Albania that is fully separated from the communist legacy.'

In reality, she acknowledged, people did not have much understanding of the details and generally expected that EU membership would bring them great benefits such as a rise in the standard of living.

'When the people started protesting against communism, the big slogan was; "we want Albania to be like Europe". It's very symbolically strong. It seemed to the people that

we were detached from Europe because of these aggres-
sive regimes and we needed to go back, rejoin the family.'

Back at the hostel, Ilir was struggling with the demands of
living in a would-be modern state. One afternoon, three
large men had appeared in reception and an argument
broke out. They were so much taller than Ilir that he was
obliged to look up at them as he made his points. He was
talking unusually energetically. In the next room, I felt like
a child, disturbed by the anger I was hearing but unable to
understand its cause. Who were these men? Debt-collec-
tors? Or members of Albania's criminal class who had
some hold over Ilir? Voices rose and fell. At times it
sounded as if an agreement was being reached, but every
time there was a lull, it was followed by a new volley of
words. Realising the dispute was not going to end any
time soon, I retreated to the garden where everyone else
was waiting for the men to leave.

'They keep coming,' explained a resident volunteer. 'If the
tax inspectors find a problem – and they always do – they
can fine you. If that happens twice in a row, they close you
down for a month and put red tape around the building.
People who are rich or know the right people don't get
closed down. One day you see a place with red tape and
the next, it's open again. Someone's made a phone call.'

Time passed. We stared at our devices in silence. A rotund
tax inspector came out into the garden, pointed a camera
at us and disappeared back into the house.

It was an hour before Ilir emerged, looking older but
visibly relieved. 'Success!' he pronounced. There would be

no fine this time, unlike the last spot inspection which had cost him four hundred euros. The problem had been that only four of the seven guests were registered in the payment book, ignoring the fact that people sometimes paid when they left in the morning. The taxmen had initially believed some of the volunteers to be paying guests and were photographing us as evidence. The situation wasn't helped by a staff member forgetting to enter some transactions. 'What can I do about this?' Ilir spread his hands indignantly.

A few days later, when I was on shift at the bar, he came out to vent his frustration. He had been to the tax office to complain about the previous fine. 'They take my money,' he fumed.

In Albania, every transaction was supposed to be recorded and a receipt filed at the tax office. There was a machine to do this on the desk at reception but the tax men wanted Ilir to install a second machine at the bar to record the takings for coffee and drinks. 'But if I add these together, and pay all the taxes, it looks like it's not worth it,' he went on. 'For the same money, I could work eight hours a day, with two days off, and with less responsibility.

'I would like some time to myself,' he added reflectively.

He'd kept the hostel open during the winter 'to maintain the vibe'. There were no guests, but he and the longterm volunteers would cook and eat together. It looked like Ilir was running a kind of commune, the summer trade keeping it going year-round. The long-term volunteers earned a share of the income from special projects. 'When people say the work is too much for them, I listen, and we change things'. At the same time, it was clear that the hostel provided an experience that was both cheap and beautiful for the international travellers who passed through its doors. Many of them left with a starry-eyed expression they hadn't had on arrival.

'To make this work, I have to do the computing, the finances, the publicity – everything,' he continued. 'I'm not good at that and it sucks all my time and energy. There are other things I want to do with my life, and if it takes all my energy, I can't do them.'

He was vague about what exactly these other things were, but it sounded as if he was talking about the kind of personal development common in the West. 'For the first time, I want to look inside,' he confided. 'I know a lot of people who feel like this. But I never used to think like this. Do you know Alan Watts?'

Then his thoughts returned to the difficulties of running the hostel: 'The problem is the taxes.'

In a modern society, everybody has to pay taxes, I told him.

'I don't want to give them my money. They take it and put it in their pockets.'

He had another hostel in the south, he added resentfully; maybe he would give this one up and go there.

'You still have to pay taxes,' I pointed out.

'I will pay rent.' This was said with finality.

'Even if you are self-employed, you have to pay tax.'

He shot me A Look. 'Then I get out of the system.'

'Okay, so you can go and live in the Albanian countryside, maybe get a tent. It's difficult to do that in Britain but I imagine it's easier here ...'

'But I want to participate!' he interrupted, adding sulkily: 'I will give up my citizenship.'

This made me laugh. 'You can't be stateless!'

Relenting, I reassured him that many in Western society go through this kind of phase, a period when the desire to pursue dreams obscures the reality of having to earn a living and participate in society. Sometimes this was accompanied by a political innocence; my own moment of truth about taxation had come about eighteen years before, when the government I'd voted for ignored huge public protests and spent taxpayers' money on a war that turned out to be based on a lie. I'd never felt the same about taxation or government since.

'Eighteen years ago?' Ilir stared.

'Yes!' I laughed. 'Catch up!'

'Extended adolescence,' he muttered in agreement.

Deep down I realised that Ilir's concerns weren't just about his own process of maturation. They also shed light on some of the dark realities of the modern world, the fact that development and modernisation involved a loss of the natural, the human and the local, and the growth of powerful forces. Ilir had chosen tourism because he wanted to show people his city, the Tirana he loved so much. 'Now they are building towers,' he fulminated. 'It is changing.'

To cheer him up, I shared what had dominated my thoughts since my visit to the art gallery. For nearly half a

century, Albania had been a closed country, all its inhabitants subordinate to the whims of a single paranoid man.
And yet now I could fly into the capital and stand along-
side a young Albanian laughing at the dictator. A miracle
had come to pass!

On the borders of the Lana and in the parks of Tirana, the trees were coming into leaf. I was familiar with the gradual progress of spring in northern Europe and the sudden jump from winter to warmth in hot countries. But this was something else, an unfolding that was both delicate and deliberate. The greening of the limes and sycamores softened the unruly facades of the buildings and the chestnuts were already displaying candlestick blooms. I realised I was falling in love with this, the strangest of cities. While I was getting familiar with its streets, it retained the peculiar atmosphere I'd noticed on my first day, a quality that belonged neither to East nor West and an energy that ran both warm and cool. Although I no longer fell over or was rendered open-jawed by what I saw, I still walked about the city in a state of mild bemusement.

Sometimes I took Riza with me on my walks. Despite her lack of regular exercise, she led a privileged life compared to most dogs in Tirana. Pets were a new thing in Albania: historically almost no one could afford to feed extra mouths and there was little knowledge of how to look after domestic companions. Yet I saw stray dogs everywhere, the yellow tags on their ears indicating they'd been vaccinated and neutered by the authorities. They wandered aimlessly along the road or slumped in shop doorways, some looking hopeless in the way of the human homeless. They were another of the city's unresolved problems, caught between the conflicting attitudes of its human residents. Many people were frightened of them, and the mayor had promised to Do Something. But nothing, apart from the circulation of rumours of dogs being rounded up and killed, had happened. Animal-loving activists, meanwhile, had opened a shelter, keeping the location secret for fear of the dogs' enemies coming to poison them.

While by no means a reformed animal, Riza had become more tractable and now responded to my voice. My Albanian vocabulary had expanded to four words which included 'Ulu!', the imperative for 'sit', and she would. With the warmer weather, I liked to sit down outside and watch the world go by. Sitting and waiting was an activity that Riza understood and tolerated – up to a point. She would sit in a state of hyper-alertness until the impulse to move got too much. From then on, a series of tugs and whines informed me that we needed to go. It turned out that she was not as brave as she appeared: seeing a couple of dogs playing with their owner in Rinia Park, she shot behind a tree in a show of fear, whimpering that she wanted Home.

~

One bright morning, I headed north of the hostel into unfamiliar streets. I was going to meet some student activists to talk about the concerns that had led to the largest protest since the fall of communism.

Some thirty years earlier, students had been central to bringing about the end of the one-party state in Albania. Student City sat on a hilltop in the southeast of the city, a complex of concrete dormitories in which the students of Tirana huddled together, suffering power cuts and water shortages. In October 1990, a bit of honest talk about the quality of the student canteen – 'the food is bad – do you agree?' developed into a protest about the conditions in which the students lived. They were joined by academics, factory workers and professionals who saw a natural alliance in the fight against the social injustice all around them. By December, the protest had evolved into a full-blown democracy movement with the slogan 'We want Albania like all Europe!' at its heart. President Ramiz Alia agreed to allow the formation of independent political parties and the following March, multi-party elections ended forty-five years of communist rule.

Almost three decades on, while Enver Hoxha University had been renamed the University of Tirana, the students were still having a bad time. Living conditions in the student accommodation had not improved and, on top of that, rising tuition fees meant that students needed to work. But the pay for their shifts in the bars and restaurants of Tirana was low, leaving them little time to study. A series of street protests and online events in December 2018 escalated and, once more, the students were joined by disenchanted citizens.

Organizata Politike – the Political Organisation – was formed in 2011 in the wake of an anti-government protest which had left four people dead. A left-wing organisation focusing on workers' rights, public education and social justice, it charged members a small proportion of their income to join, with students paying a nominal fee. The social centre it ran was a godsend to the students of Tirana, providing them with a much-needed place to meet.

I had no difficulty in finding the Logu social centre, a two-storeyed white building with a balcony of bright red. It was set in a generous patio where students clustered in small groups, chatting energetically. I soon found the contacts I'd arranged to meet. Mirela, a flame-haired young woman who lived in Student City, was doing a Masters in sociology which she couldn't complete because she didn't have the money for the fees. Bespectacled Flavia was in her first year studying economics and privileged in comparison with the average student: she lived with her parents who had agreed to support her through her studies. At first, she had gone out to work but soon found her eight-hour shifts at the bakery too much. The experience had given her a sense of solidarity with her fellow students who often did night shifts before going to lectures in the morning.

The young women were clearly good friends, all-but finishing each other's sentences as they took it in turns to explain the students' grievances. The origins of the recent protests, said Mirela, went back several years to government reforms which had redirected public funds to private universities.

'And the funny thing was the people who profit from this law are businessmen,' said Flavia, adding that the government had shown no interest in how the policy would affect education. Then, against a background of rising tuition fees, the government had decided to impose a new fee for retaking exams. The students had pointed out that the struggle to make ends meet made it difficult to pass all the modules the first time; sometimes work commitments prevented them from even sitting the exams. When the protests first began, the government's response was to insult the protestors, claiming they were 'the people who don't learn, the bad students'.

I was beginning to recognise this as a feature of public discourse in Albania. When there was an obvious problem in society, the groups affected were labelled 'bad', leaving the real issue unaddressed. It was classic victim-blaming and scapegoating.

'They don't understand that a student has to work and that it's impossible to be a very good student in these conditions,' added Flavia.

'I think they understand that,' said Mirela. 'They know what they are doing to our education but they don't care. They wanted society to be against the students, to say "they are bad students".' Some of the smearing had come from the Prime Minister himself, who had used his social media platforms to label the students 'dummies'.

The protests grew and by February 2019 an estimated hundred thousand people – a huge number in a small country – had joined the anti-government protest in front of the Ministry of Education. In an echo of the negotiations with Alia three decades before, Rama asked to meet a group of students. This time, the students refused; they had made clear what they wanted. The requests were repeated, to no avail. 'One of the strongest points of the protest was we don't want to negotiate,' explained Flavia.

I was impressed. The young activists would not allow themselves to be dragged into a confusing situation with seasoned politicians who would try to manipulate them. They wanted a cut in tuition fees, student involvement in decision-making about the sector and investment in Student City. It sounded as if they were doing the thinking the policymakers were failing to do and trying to bring much-needed reforms to the country's dysfunctional higher education system. 'My dad is fifty-five years old and stayed in the same dormitories in the 1980s,' said Flavia. 'He's like "that's the closet, the bed I left!" Nothing has changed since then. There are rats; the walls are in terrible condition, and so are the bathrooms.'

The rent was so expensive that three students often shared a single room. 'For three people, you have three beds, a table, a closet and a sink,' explained Mirela. 'We don't have heating and sometimes there's no water. You don't have a place to wash your clothes or cook. We use one sink for cleaning our teeth, washing the dishes, our clothes – everything.'

'What is the effect of all this on young people, their work prospects, and on society in general?' I asked.

The men tended to emigrate, said Mirela, leaving the women behind. Higher education was particularly important for women in Albania, as it provided the only real route to independence. 'Women in Albania don't have another choice,' added Flavia. 'If you study you have the opportunity to have a job and to be independent, or you will be married. For example, if I don't go to high school, my parents will say "you will be married now. What will you do at home?"'

Their parents' generation tended to be supportive of the protests. They had seen how the student protests of 1990 had brought about the fall of the communist regime; now, middle-aged and disillusioned, they hoped that, with corruption and dysfunction continuing under a new political system, the same would happen again. 'The people believe that the students will be in power, create a new alternative,' said Mirela. 'They believe it so much.'

'When we were marching in the streets, there were people saying from their windows and balconies, "we have hopes in you, we hope you will change something",' added Flavia. 'There were very high expectations.'

'We know that this kind of protest will not change a lot,' said Mirela. 'It's just a moment. But it's the moment when you start to see another way, for society.'

The students' success in attracting widespread support and generating hopes for an all-encompassing political movement had drawn the interest of the political opposition. 'This is very good, but we don't want political parties in our protest,' said Mirela calmly.

'Because these protests were being used by the Democratic Party,' continued Flavia. 'The moment we would accept them the Prime Minister would be like, "this is the same thing, it's all organised by the Opposition" and it would have lost its meaning.'

'My family and friends say "create a party",' said Mirela. 'But we need to go step by step, to give hope to the people and after that, create a structure. Because it's not just mobilisation, you need a structure in society that will be strong so that it doesn't matter who comes into power.'

'You have to get the system by the roots,' agreed Flavia. A new political party by itself wasn't going to bring about change; what was needed was a new political system and culture. 'But that takes time.'

'It cannot be only the students; we don't have the power,' said Mirela. 'We need to change the way our society functions. The alternative will not come from the top.'

'Change will come from the bottom,' said Flavia. 'To build a party that brings a true change, you have to work on the ground. That's why we have to work first with workers and small businesses. We have to get people conscious of the situation and then maybe form political parties.'

Listening to the two young women, I was amazed at their political maturity. Flavia was eighteen; Mirela only a few years older. They did not come from activist families, nor had they experience of political movements in other times or places. Yet somehow they had an innate understanding of power dynamics and the nature of the challenge they faced.

'Where did you get the idea to do all this from?' I asked.

'I don't know!' smiled Mirela.

We left the mystery hanging in the air, and the pair showed me around the centre. Downstairs in the basement was an events space for screening films, poetry readings and presentations by students and academics. Sometimes public events were held to raise money for running costs. The place was a mixture of student union, cultural centre and library, facilities commonly available to students in the

West but unknown in Tirana. 'We are trying to create a place where we can debate about social problems, working spaces, This kind of social centre is something new in Albania. People are sometimes doubtful about it,' said Mirela.

We went upstairs to the study room. A shelf of books marked 'Filozofike/Politike' lent it a library-like atmosphere, but it was the megaphones on the window sill that drew my attention. Mirela picked up a red one, and Flavia a cream one. 'These are our guns,' said Mirela, handling hers lovingly. In the street protests, those supporting the government had expensive amplifiers to broadcast their message. Yet with just five megaphones between them, the students had made more of an impact. The police were nice to them, saying: "our kids are students. We are with you".

The issues facing the young activists of the Organizata Politike were legion. 'We don't know what to work on,' said Mirela. 'This morning we heard that people's houses were being demolished to make way for a new road and the police were beating them. We could go and have a look if you like.'

The three of us set off across town.

The demolition zone was in the Bregu i Lumit area to the northeast of the city. A number of houses were being pulled down to make way for a new road near the site of the former railway station. The New Boulevard, technically an extension of the existing boulevard that ran through the centre of the city, was key to the plans the

Prime Minister and mayor had for Tirana, a vision which aimed to limit urban sprawl and pack the city's growing population into high-density developments.

There was just one problem. Thirty-eight houses stood in the path of the new road, family homes built after the fall of communism when no planning laws were in place. A process to give them legal status had subsequently been established and most of their owners had embarked on it, submitting documents and paying fees to the authorities. But when the plans for the New Boulevard were announced, the Prime Minister cancelled the legal process and denied the owners compensation. The previous week, bulldozers had come at daybreak and begun knocking down the houses. The police had fired tear gas on the residents and arrested those who were put up a real resistance. Journalists, meanwhile, had been prevented from entering the area and taking pictures.

The part of the city we were walking through had a suburban sameness, its straight streets bordered by beige apartment blocks. Mirela led us into a small bakery and bought us all byrek for lunch, waving aside my attempt to give her some money. My first packet of pastry was filled with a tomato paste both rich and juicy, while my second was tightly packed with cheese and oniony-sweet, the most delicious byrek I'd had so far. Munching, we resumed our journey. 'I don't know how far it is,' said Mirela.

More walking, more apartment blocks. Then suddenly it was clear we'd entered the zone of the New Boulevard. A wide grey road stretched emptily ahead of us, bounded by metal fencing. The paving stones underfoot were new, new, new and there was almost no one else in sight. Beside the pavement, pieces of canvas stretched over the metal fencing displayed the architectural plans for the project. The first, headed Tirana Bulevardi I Ri, depicted the road as a thick green line cutting through the existing city with its mess of little streets. Shiny buildings, leafy walkways and well-dressed young professionals adorned the following canvases. But behind the fencing, I could see the houses of the current residents: ramshackle affairs among lines of washing and untended gardens.

We continued our promenade along the pristine boulevard. It was a cloudy day and the sky echoed the greyness of the road; it felt as if we could walk into this grey world forever. And then it all came to an end. Ahead of us pallets of concrete blocks and signage prohibiting entry indicated that we were approaching the construction site. Somehow Mirela knew where to go, leading us unhesitatingly off to the right, onto a path on higher ground that shadowed the roadworks. As we walked along it, the signs of construction intensified. Pallets of concrete filled the space below as far as the eye could see. The surviving houses on the other side looked so close to the works that I wondered how their inhabitants managed. The path became nothing more than a dirt track edged by vegetation and piles of dumped rubbish. Snaking round to the left, it took us into the edge of the demolition zone. A woman and a boy were walking over some rubble, attempting to bring some order to the remains of their former home. Their expressions were such that we did not linger to talk. We continued until we found ourselves on a ridge of earth that traversed the course of the new road and found ourselves overlooking an extraordinary scene.

The destruction took my breath away. An enormous pile of rubble rose amid a tangle of freshly-felled trees, a column of granite smoke curling slowly up out of the pile. The dust had not yet settled. A male figure was moving over it, apparently trying to pull things out of the jumble of concrete and piping. Near him, a woman stood with her back to us, staring ahead.

I had seen houses bulldozed by Israeli forces in the West Bank and entire suburbs reduced to rubble in Lebanon. But there was something about this scene that made it extremely hard to take in. No military conflict had taken place; the destruction was the result of building contractors destroying people's homes at the command of a democratically-elected government. Our vantage point provided a clear view of the contrast between creation and destruction: in the foreground were rafts of fresh grey concrete and the kind of bench featured in architectural drawings. Behind it rose a huge mound of soil and, beyond that, was the next house in the path of the road, a square of yellow ochre with its back half collapsed, as if it had been hit by a torpedo. A cloud of smoke rose in front of it.

We hardly spoke as we picked our way across the ridge of no-man's land. Over on the other side, we found ourselves looking down into the yard of a recently-demolished house. A tall man in late middle age was plastering around the door frame of a shed; another man was standing outside a tumble-down shack. The men were friendly and a conversation quickly developed, with Mirela and Flavia translating the main points for me. The tall man's house had been bulldozed a few days ago; he and his family had lived there for twenty-seven years and the process of regularising its legal status had been well underway. Now that the house had gone, he was converting an outbuilding into a mini-home so that his family would have somewhere to go when they were released from prison. He gestured to the shack opposite: 'He wants to live there but it's not possible'. His friend had slept there for the past few nights but now the rains had come it was leaking. With its loosely-laid corrugated roofing and walls of mismatched planks, the shack looked as if it was barely holding together.

Accepting the man's invitation to come down into his yard, we picked our way down to street level and went round to the metal gates on the other side. He showed us, with a degree of pride, the inside of the building he was working on: there was neat bare space that could become a tiny living room and, beside it, a door opened onto a shiny new sink and toilet. With new people to talk to, the man gave free rein to his rage: 'We have been invaded by the Serbs and Turks but they had mercy for women and children. This state doesn't care. The government is fighting its own people; it's killing its own people,' Mirela and Flavia murmured sympathetically. 'Only a fascist government would do this,' continued the man. 'Enver Hoxha was a dictator but when there was an accident, he helped people.'

We said our thanks and left the man to his work. From ground level, it was clear that the thirty-eight houses had been almost a village, with generous houses and gardens set along a dirt track, the hills rising behind. We made our way along the track to the large ochre house we'd seen from a distance. From the front it looked almost normal. A large van was parked in the drive and its owners were busy loading it with whatever they could salvage from the back of the house. Window frames, doors – all these things cost money and could be used in a new build elsewhere, my companions explained. A grim-faced woman told us the back had been bulldozed that morning; the rest of the house would go tomorrow. 'We are mourning,' she said.

A bit further along, we found a group of people clustered around a small shop. An animated discussion of the day's events was taking place. A young woman had just returned from the police station; the rest of her household were still in hospital as a result of the tear gas pumped into their house before it was bulldozed.

We began our walk back to the city centre, passing a lacquered wooden headboard that had been left at the side of the track.

'The house is very important in Albania,' explained Mirela. 'It's a very difficult thing to get here. It takes a life-time, and maybe three brothers working, one in Italy, another in Germany, to get one.'

I was shocked by what I had seen on the site of the New Boulevard and what it revealed about contemporary Albania. Thanks to the students, I had got pictures and information forbidden to local journalists in a supposedly democratic society.

A few days later, Kristina Voko gave me a fuller picture of the state of press freedom. As the executive director of the Balkan Investigative Reporting Network in Albania, she and her team worked to promote freedom of speech and democratic values. BIRN ran Balkan Insight, an English-language website which published news and analysis about what was going on in the region. She told me of the struggle of doing independent journalism in a country where the politicians had little sense of objectivity or freedom and were constantly trying to interfere. When the Prime Minister read articles he didn't like, he tended to launch personal attacks on the journalists who had written them. Meanwhile, the municipal police had no scruples about preventing journalists from covering events in public space.

Tirana's mayor Erion Veliaj did not give interviews and had not held a press conference since being elected in 2015. Yet he was always in the media. 'Still you see him every day in every news edition,' explained Kristina. 'Why? Because he has a huge crew of people filming everywhere he goes and every TV station is offered images every day, prepared by the staff. But as a journalist you are not allowed to follow any of those events, even if it's a public event.

'Everything that has to do with Tirana will be delivered to you by the local government, through the eyes of local government and with very specific shots.'

🦋   6   🦋

The hostel was alive with a tale of attempted abduction.

Two of the female guests, one British, one Dutch, had been on their way to Shkoder, and subsequently planned to spend a few days in the north of Albania. They had been waiting at the bus stop for the first leg of their journey when they were befriended by a young girl. The girl struck them as odd in a way they couldn't put their finger on: she looked unkempt and yet was very friendly. There was a bus strike, she said, and a few minutes later a car pulled up. Somehow, between the girl and the driver, the young women allowed themselves to be talked into accepting a lift. Then they were all in the car together, the young girl, the driver and the two foreign women. Things got very confusing: the girl claimed not to know the driver but her demeanour suggested there was an understanding between them. At one point she was on the phone to someone else and the women heard her say: 'beautiful girls, beautiful girls'. Still the warning signals weren't strong enough. Then the car drove up to a house where a group of men was standing outside. Their collective stance conveyed anticipation and predation. The two women took one look and the penny dropped.

We were sitting in a near-circle in one of the dorms, every woman in the hostel, listening to the occupant of a lower bunk bed tell her story. The two women had fled both car and the waiting men – there was no attempt at any physical assault – and found themselves in a strange region. The Dutch woman had decided to continue her trip alone but the British woman wanted to return to the safety of the hostel. It had taken her hours to get back to Tirana and she had narrowly avoided seduction by a taxi driver who kept asking where her husband was.

The rest of us gasped and empathised, asking the odd question but mainly listening. I did the best thing I knew for a distressed English woman. When I returned with the cup of tea, the adventurer was deciding not to tell her mother about her experience. Gradually, the circle dispersed and we left her to have an early night.

A few days later, I had the opportunity to consult an expert about the incident. Imelda Poole was the President of the Mary Ward Loreto Foundation, a charity that worked with the victims of human trafficking and Albania's most vulnerable communities. A British nun in her sixties who had lived in Albania for fourteen years, she struck me as the perfect person for this kind of work: sensible and kind yet tough enough to deal with its dark side. Ana Stakaj, who ran the organisation's programme for women, had grown up in a mountain village but lived in Tirana most of her life. As we sat around a table in the foundation's meeting room, the two women helped me to make sense of what I was seeing and hearing.

'It sounds like the traffickers are becoming brave,' said Imelda when I told her about the women's experience. 'They would get a lot more for them being foreign.' Neither she nor Ana had heard of such a thing before. But they found the story quite easy to believe: Albania had a curious capacity for keeping secrets.

'When you are outside Albania, you would hear a lot about it,' explained Ana. 'When you are inside Albania, you can't. The common population wouldn't know about it because the media don't talk about it. The people who talk about it are the civil society organisations: now, because of the influence of internationals – the embassies, other governments and the UN – our government has taken some actions. But there is very little done.'

'What is the extent of the trafficking?' I asked.

'In this kind of crime, you don't have exact data,' she replied. 'It's quite hidden: if you go to a community they wouldn't talk about it because they wouldn't realise it's human trafficking. In some regions, the community would recognise the victim as a failed prostitute. This is the sadness.'

While there wasn't any definitive statistical data, added Imelda, it was clear that Albania was the number one country in Europe for human trafficking. High numbers of trafficked Albanians had been identified in the UK.

'Can you describe the process by which someone gets trafficked?'

'The most common is the lover-boy,' replied Ana. 'They tend to find a girl who looks pretty but comes from a dysfunctional family or has problems with incest. So they find this girl in the corner who is vulnerable and doesn't have many people around her.' Sometimes a neighbour in the community might introduce the trafficker to the vulnerable girl for a fee. Thereafter, a courtship led to the young woman agreeing to go abroad with her new boyfriend. Once she was in country such as Italy or Greece, she would be sold on. The trafficking had begun.

Not all trafficking was sexual; some people were manipulated into indentured labour, indebting themselves to smugglers to take them abroad on the promise of life-changing opportunities. 'They have this big dream that the UK is going to provide a job and then they will return,' said Ana. 'When they get to England, they have nothing. Boys are made to believe that if they do a job such as cannabis cultivation or car washing for, say, six months they will have paid the debt. Then they fall into petty crime.'

Meanwhile, attempts to run away or tell the authorities were kept in check by blackmail. 'They know that if they cheat in any way their families will be abused,' said Imelda. 'There's a lot of threat.' The traffickers' chains were long and closely-connected, and some smaller gangs were run by larger international ones.

Within Albania, exploitation was rife, continued Ana. Some people worked in factories that were effectively sweatshops, while university students could end up in prostitution. 'The traffickers zoom in there very fast and they blackmail them, and traffick them on.'

'What is it about Albanian society that creates this kind of environment?' I asked.

There were many reasons, she said, from the lack of good government to the poor economy and culture of endemic corruption. The geography of the country, which was sixty per cent mountainous and very rural, made for isolated communities in which wrongdoing was hard to expose. The country's history of oppression by outside powers was also a factor. 'Because of that, people are losing human values. So many years of suffering and maltreatment under communism, the Ottoman empire – it's like we never were free. At the beginning of the nineties, we thought we were free, but then the people who were running the state didn't know what they were doing. People tend to just escape. There is this tendency to say: "This is not the place I should be. I just have to go to Australia, America, the UK, Germany."'

'So trafficking didn't happen under communism?' I asked.

'No, no ...' chorused the women.

Ana elaborated: 'During communism, most of the population was protected: they had education and safety. Then after the nineties, everything was in chaos. There was democracy but there wasn't a clear understanding of democracy and what freedom means. In '97, people with guns, new-formed gangs were putting terror into society. A year of terror! By the end of '98, most of the guns were collected. Most of them were sold to the Kosovo war.'

Communism had left a legacy of distrust and, thirty years on, people still tended to conceal their emotions. 'Albanians have learnt to be protective,' said Imelda. 'I would never use the word "lying". It's a harsh word in English, but here's it's to do with protection. Ultimately you come to speak the truth, you're just finding your way to trusting enough to speak it.' There was a 'mmm' of agreement from Ana. 'It's like this way round,' Imelda made circles with her hand. 'It's not they begin purposely with a lie. They begin with protection, knowing the truth, but feeling their way to be ready to say it. I don't understand it truly, but I understand the process.'

The Palace of Dreams by Albania's best known novelist Ismail Kadare captured the psychological effects of the surveillance system under the dictatorship. 'He wrote about truth for us in a way we know,' said Ana. 'Fear, and poverty, and isolation closed the mind, causing it to go in a circle and malfunction. In communism, people were forced even to spy on their brother, and the wife on their husband. The way communism was done here in Albania destroyed human values. There was a lot of propaganda about values but at the same time, people were afraid that someone would tell them off. So they learned to keep things private and secret, especially thoughts: your thoughts are always secret.'

'We had people spying even for books,' she continued. 'My father was almost sent to prison just for having some books. Thank God there were also people who were good, even if they were in power, and they said "just get rid of the books". The books ended up in the nearby river, so he was saved.'

The women also shed some light on the lives of the disabled. I was getting used to seeing people with extreme disabilities on the streets of Tirana, but one man whose body was composed of just a torso, as if sliced off at the pelvis, disturbed me. The half man stood on the pavement in the city centre begging. Something in my stomach jumped up to my heart every time I passed him.

The man I'd seen on my first day dragging a useless leg along the pavement was probably on the street due a form of trafficking, Imelda explained. He might be living at home but, with the agreement of his family, taken to the street by a gang who took a cut of whatever he collected from begging. She often used to see a legless girl of about eighteen tumbled off a motorbike onto the pavement to beg. Passing one day, she'd found a group of men peeing on her. She'd intervened to scatter them but never saw the girl again.

Having a mentally disabled child in the family was a source of shame, added Ana. There would be no attempt to diagnose or understand a condition such as autism. The parents would simply label their child handicapped and try to marry them off, a disabled woman to another disabled man but a disabled man to a normal woman.

I was off to visit the Valdete Trust, a charity providing education for disabled young people. The project was pioneering: in Albania, disabled children did not usually go to school, even after a law passed in 2014 gave them the right to education. The charity had been founded after a British woman called Sue Davidson met Valdete Gjonpali who had developed cerebral palsy as an infant and was facing a lifetime confined to the family home. Sue had raised funds to fly Valdete to the UK and have surgery which would potentially enable her to walk. Then, determined to do something for more disabled people in a country she loved, Sue set up a day centre offering lessons and physiotherapy to a small number of young people suffering from degenerative conditions in the Tirana area.

The centre was in a village near the town of Vore, a bus ride about half an hour away from the capital. It was the first time I'd been out of Tirana and I studied the landscape filing past the window with interest. The suburbs resembled the outskirts of a Middle Eastern city: a long, dusty road lined with cheaply-built apartment blocks, industrial buildings and garages. Before long, the scenery became rural and I was looking out at green hills dotted with chalet-style houses. The pastoral scene was only slightly marred by a giant Pepsi hoarding halfway up the hillside.

The bus pulled up in a pleasant street lined with newish buildings painted pastel shades. We had arrived in Vore. Deciding to get my bearings before ringing to be picked up, I walked down the main street and turned, on a whim, into a side road. Neatly parked was a minibus with 'The Valdete Trust' on its side. Mondi the driver was already waiting for me.

Mondi drove back out of town and along some winding country roads until we arrived at a large modern house with 'Valdete' emblazoned above the door. On the patio outside, a group of young adults was sitting around a table in the shade of some trees. They were all in wheel-chairs. A member of staff introduced me and disappeared back into the house. Beside Erblin, a broad-shouldered young man, sat a woman with fashionably-cut black hair and an immaculately made-up face. Valdete's radiant smile sent a thought through my mind: *if I was younger and didn't know better, I'd mistake that smile for that of someone who finds life easy. But these days I know that smiles can hide many things.*

The young people were eager to talk. Erblin had been coming to the centre for nearly five years. At the age of ten, he had gone to live in a residential centre but left seven years later without any qualifications. It was considered pointless for disabled children to do exams because it was assumed they would not participate in society; mainstream schools didn't even have accessible toilets. But in his early twenties, Erblin had resumed his education at Valdete. He reeled off the subjects he was studying with pride: English, Albanian, Chemistry, Physics, Maths, Geography, and History. He would sit the national exams.

'It means we will get qualifications like everybody else, and maybe go to university in the future,' explained Valdete.

She, too, had missed a lot of schooling. As a child, she had gone to a day centre that was well resourced but did not provide education. Meeting Sue at the age of sixteen had changed the course of her life. 'I had a dream,' she smiled. 'I saw God saying "stand up because I will hold you". I stood up and walked. By his side were two angels. In the morning I told Sue. She went to Britain but told me not to lose hope.'

It had been difficult to persuade her parents to let a stranger take charge of her health, but Valdete visited Sue in Scotland to explore the possibility of surgery. The following year, she spent eight months in Britain having a series of operations. After one of them she regained consciousness wreathed in smiles. 'The doctor said: "how weird. You wake up and you are smiling". He had warned her that even after all the surgery was finished, there was a risk she would remain paralysed. Nearly a decade on, she was walking with a zimmer frame or a bit of help from her mother and sister.

'Here it's good because people are committed to each other and we know each other. We are all pleased with the school,' she smiled. 'For a disabled person like me, it's a dream. People will say: "You go to school? But you are disabled." People would be "wow", even today. In Albania, it's very hard. Because if you are disabled, you are stupid. They look at us like we are animals. There are no ramps and when I go in the street there's no path.'

In future, she hoped to go to university and have a family and home of her own. 'And to have a job.' She nodded towards the golden device in front of me and flashed: 'Like you I can do computer!'

Erblin displayed a similar feistiness. If he wasn't able to finish his education, he said, he would spend his time 'fighting with the government' for access to services for disabled people.

'You're sporty,' I nodded at his shoulders.

'Yes.' He seemed pleased at this acknowledgement of his physical strength. He played pingpong and football; the previous year he'd taken part in a marathon using a smaller, lighter wheelchair. After he finished his education, he hoped to find a job, perhaps in computing or something to do with phones.

Both he and Valdete still experienced prejudice on a daily basis. 'People see us as disabled people in wheelchairs and think that we should not go out and not see the sun and not enjoy life.'

'We want to be normal,' said Valdete.

'We want to be strong and independent,' agreed Erblin. 'In Europe and America they know more how to treat disabled people and show them love and respect. When I go out with my mother, policemen say, "oh no, it's not allowed". Every day I fight with them. In their mind I am a stupid kid. But I am a person!'

'I fight with my family for my rights,' said Valdete. 'Before, they said to me, "why do you have to go outside? Why do you need to go to school?" I have to fight for everything. You have to show them that you want to exist in the world.'

The third person round the table had had an even more difficult start in life than her companions. Egla had muscular dystrophy and would be thirty-three in the summer. But until she started coming to Valdete five years before, she had never left the house. 'I was always at home. My friends came to the house, I watched TV. Then my mind changed because I thought, "okay, I have to go out. I am not locked in the house".'

It was lunchtime and I asked the centre manager if I could stay. I didn't want to dash away like the stereotypical journalist: there was something magical about sitting with these spirited young people on this balmy spring day. She seemed pleased: if I could wait till the end of the school day, I could have a lift back to Tirana as the bus deposited the students at their various homes.

Getting the students up into the house to join the others after the morning's lessons was a gruelling operation. The building had no lift or stairlift: it was rented and could not be adapted, so each person had to be taken from their wheelchair and strapped into a special seat. Mondi then hauled them up two flights of stairs, a step at a time, and on the first floor they returned to their wheelchair which had been carried upstairs separately. Lunch was a simple, plentiful affair of stew with bread and fruit and the mood at the table convivial. Afterwards, the trio I'd been talking to disappeared into classrooms and I went back downstairs to work at a table outside.

Just as I was settling down to write some notes, a new person approached, manoeuvring her slight, asymmetrical body with the support of a teacher. Her twisted face was smiling shyly and her gaze intensely focused on me. 'Do you want to talk to Alex?' asked the teacher.

But in what language? The newcomer had almost no English and I no Albanian. I offered her the languages I did speak and her face lit up at the suggestion of Spanish. And so we made our way through a conversational dance, exchanging pieces of information in the semi-formal courtesy of country dancers, my partner ending some of her answers with a colloquial flourish – 'tu sabes' – sometimes repeating my phrases for the delight of saying them herself. She had taught herself the language by watching Spanish programmes on television. 'I am twenty-one,' she volunteered. 'And I am five.' But the content of our dialogue was by the bye: this was about the joy of participating in a wider world of communication.

There was a final conversation to have before the day was done. Anneco was the live-in house matron and had long experience of Albania. A missionary from Holland, she had seen how attitudes had changed since she first visited the country in 1996, when families would hide the disabled in their homes. 'I knew immediately this is the place I want to be,' she said. 'I fell in love with the Albanian people and I am still in love.'

'Why?' I asked. I understood and was mystified at the same time.

'I don't know why I love them because they are not easy,' she replied. 'They are warm, very hospitable, very good at problem solving. But they lie a lot; they lie about everything.'

She paused for a moment, then added: 'I'm not angry with them about that because it's to with their history, with survival and habit. This is a culture of shame and honour – to save your honour, you can lie. It's so important you are honourable you will do anything. For example, the other day I was in the car with an Albanian woman and her aunt rang. She said: "I can't speak now – I'm at the doctor's".'

The bus made its way back to Tirana via various towns and villages, depositing the students at their homes. Each stop brought the onerous business of getting a person out of the bus and lowered safely onto the pavement. Mondi looked tired and so did Valdete. I myself no longer felt like talking.

'It is tiring,' smiled Valdete, reading my mind as I watched Mondi struggle to get a wheelchair containing a sizeable person onto the ramp. Her smile was both bright and sad. 'But it is good for us. Better than staying in the house.'

❀   7   ❀

The weather in Tirana had turned April-strange, the skies delivering sudden downpours of torrential rain. There was a hailstorm the like of which I had never seen, with lumps of ice the size of olives. They bombarded the hostel patio, bouncing off the tables and the roof of the bar. We huddled under the verandas and stared at the scene in front of us, open-mouthed.

The following Saturday there was going to be a protest in The Boulevard outside the Prime Minister's Office. Edvin puffed excitedly on his cigarette as he told me about it. The past couple of months had seen a number of demonstrations, with protestors calling for the socialist prime minister to quit over alleged corruption and election fraud, the installation of a transitional government and electoral reform followed by general elections. As Opposition, the Democratic Party had a clear interest in playing a leading role in the protests. But the unrest recalled the pro-democracy demonstrations of the 1990s and suggested the possibility of real change.

I would go, I told Edvin. He nodded; it was an obvious thing for a visiting writer to do. The police were likely to use tear gas, he warned, so it was important that I take a scarf to cover my face. And when things got heated, the crowd tended to move in waves, forwards and backwards. His advice made sense. I'd been to protests in many countries and had some hair-raising experiences.

Standing nearby, Ilir looked thoughtful. 'You are going to this?' he asked. Yes, I told him firmly.

Saturday morning dawned and Ilir asked if I was still going to the protest. I repeated that I was.

'I think I will come with you.'

'Okay,' I nodded.

Secretly, I was delighted. It was gratifying, having entered the life of the hostel so wholeheartedly, to find this willingness to enter my very different world of observation and reporting. While I wasn't exactly scared of going to a Balkan protest alone, a supportive male presence would be most welcome. And from a journalistic point of view, it was better to enter an unfamiliar situation with a local contact who could interpret things.

By early afternoon, it was pouring again. Ilir put on some shoes and readied his bicycle. I expressed some doubt about whether it was a good idea to take a bicycle on a protest but soon realised I was onto a loser and stopped talking. We agreed, on the other hand, that an umbrella would be a useful addition and he fetched a large one from the hostel lobby.

We made our way up Kavaja Street, Ilir wheeling his bicycle along the pavement beside me. The road was full of people walking purposefully towards to Skanderbeg Square. They were an intensified version of Tirana's usual street population dressed in black, grey and navy but, on this day, many of them were carrying identical umbrellas with a blue and white logo. The umbrellas were effectively the banners of the Democratic Party.

'This is what I don't like. It's mostly men,' remarked Ilir. 'The women stay at home with the children. There may be tear gas, and no one wants children in that.'

The explanation didn't quite make sense. Most protests I'd been on had plenty of women, especially young and older women. But there was almost none in this crowd.

A big crowd was gathering in Skanderbeg Square. At Ilir's suggestion, we mounted the steps of the National Museum and surveyed the scene below. The crowd stood with its back to us, facing The Boulevard, the blacks and greys alleviated by the odd pink and red umbrella. People stood in clusters, chatting and examining their smartphones. The men stood with in overtly masculine stance, their legs planted firmly apart. The air held a strange mixture of anticipation and purposelessness; the mood wasn't like that of any demo I had ever been on.

'Do you want to go to the Prime Minister's Office?' asked Ilir. He was hoping I'd say "no, I've seen enough" and we could return to the hostel, mission somewhat accomplished. But I was entranced by this strange world and curious as to what form the energy would take when things crystallised.

The crowd was starting to move off down The Boulevard. Crossing the square, we followed them past the red Ministry of Urban Development into the administrative quarter. A line of policemen waited expressionlessly behind some metal barricades. The rain had eased off and it was pleasant walking in the road; our middle course afforded a good view of the pine trees and elegant buildings. Ilir pointed to a group holding a banner with the words MBRO TEATRIN in big blue letters. It belonged, he explained, to the group who were protesting against the proposed demolition of the national theatre. The Teatri Kombëtar building was considered an exceptional example of Italian futurism, but in 2018 a Danish architectural firm had won a government contract to build a new national theatre shaped like a bow tie and scheduled the current building for demolition.

At the other end of The Boulevard a big crowd was amassing. But around us there were only a few people and the proceedings had acquired a festive air. There were stands selling refreshments at the side of the street and a pair of huge speakers were booming Balkan rock. For me, the atmosphere was becoming comfortably familiar, like that of a rock concert. We, the people of the street, were going to a gig together. Ilir noticed my obvious enjoyment. 'It's not all smiley, you know,' he reproved.

Horns were blaring from the crowd in front of the Prime Minister's Office. Ilir quailed slightly. 'I don't like this noise,' he said. 'I don't even go to the stadium any more.'

'Come on,' I urged.

The music coming from the speakers was mesmerising. Its vocals and beat had a power I'd not heard even in the heaviest metal. It looped seductively, the same notes repeated with growing intensity and drama. The music, Ilir told me, was by an Albanian band called Jericho and the current track happened to be his favourite. His mood lightened momentarily and he darted over to a nearby stand, returning with a paper bag. 'I love these,' he said, cracking open the shell of a sunflower seed with his teeth and nibbling on the contents.

As we approached the Prime Minister's Office the crowd thickened and the air above people's heads was full of smoke. Clouds of white vapour and thick coils of granite drifted over the blue umbrellas and the sound of explosions added to the horns. I chose a spot with a good view of the office behind the bulk of the crowd and by a side street. We could easily make a quick getaway if we needed to.

The Prime Minister's Office was surprisingly nondescript, a big block of beige, the cream shutters on its windows drawn down. I must have passed it many times without noticing, a dull administrative buildings that was closed for business today. But on the roof a row of dark figures stood poised. Snipers. A couple of TV vans were parked in front of us, their roofs bearing men with tripods. The cameras were trained on the building.

The pops and bangs were increasing. They generated smoke of many shades of grey and, for the first time, black.

'Why the black smoke?' I asked.

'To look menacing,' replied Ilir.

Cries of RAMA IK! RAMA IK! were rising, in deep, male voices, from the crowd,. 'What does it mean?' I asked.

'Rama go.'

A volley of particularly loud explosions shattered the air.

'They are trying to provoke,' said Ilir. 'I want to go. I don't like this.'

'Just a bit longer,' I pleaded.

Splodges of blue were appearing on the cream facade of the Prime Minister's Office; the protestors were throwing paint bombs. To get a better look at what was happening in the crowd, I got up on the stone edging a nearby building. Ilir waited by a signpost, holding his bicycle protectively against him. Every now and then he cast me a reproachful look.

Another explosion. And then another.

Ilir sent me a single, deliberate blink. I got down from my plinth and rejoined him at the signpost.

A man in the heart of the crowd was giving a speech. What was Democratic Party leader Lulzim Basha saying?

Ilir sounded weary as he replied: 'That they are criminals who are destroying … ' he searched for the word.

'… the country …' I supplied. The political rhetoric was near-universal.

A large torpedo-shaped object flew over the crowd and burst into flames.

'That one's illegal,' said Ilir. 'One more big like that, and the police will react.'

A number of black and blue splodges now decked the facade of the Prime Minister's Office. Ilir grasped the handlebars of his bicycle. He had made a decision. 'Will you come with me?'

I would. This demonstration was unlike any I had been to. I could feel a dark energy gathering force and Ilir's nervousness was infectious.

The side road took us swiftly away from the protest. We made a leisurely way back through the city, a visibly-relaxed Ilir pointing out some personal sights. There, in that impressive house and garden set back from the road he used to play with a childhood friend. The city felt calm again.

Then, with enough distance between us and the shouting, throwing, exploding crowd, I shared what was on my mind.

'I know there's a darkness here. The first night I came here, to Tirana, I felt that energy, of the darkness. I didn't like it.'

Ilir nodded. Yes, that was how it was.

We had circled our way back round and were re-entering Skanderbeg Square. Both of us started laughing. There, on the plinth of the Skanderbeg Monument was a lone demonstrator, a tubby figure dressed in black, his fist raised aloft. We waved and smiled at him and he smiled back. Somehow, we all understood that this was a different kind of protest, one that lacked the aggression of what we'd just witnessed while clearly standing up for Humanity.

It was raining again, and the paving stones gleamed as we navigated our way across the square, managing bicycle and umbrella. Five minutes later, the red-tiled wall of the hostel came into view.

'Home sweet home', said Ilir with audible relief.

~

It was nearly two days before I found the time to return to the Prime Minister's Office to get some pictures of the colour-bombed building. But when I got to the right part of The Boulevard, I found the cream facade pristine. Opposite were two cleaning vehicles and a group of men with the air of having just finished a job. At least I could take a couple of pictures of them. A besuited man who looked like he might be in charge gave me a searching look but said nothing.

$\maltese$ 8 $\maltese$

My time at the hostel was coming to an end. I had already extended my stay a few days but could put off leaving no longer. A friend was coming to visit and I needed a place to host her. And it was clear to me that, with its international culture and hippy vibe, the hostel was insulating me from getting a realistic picture of Tirana. Now I knew I did want to write about the hostel, both because it revealed a lot about the new Albania and because it threw its dark side into stark relief.

I went to reception to see Ilir.

'I need to talk to you about the book. I want to write about the hostel.'

He seemed pleased. 'So we will be famous.'

He had a decision to make: did he want to be named or would he prefer his identity and that of the hostel to be disguised?

'Name me.'

'You won't know exactly what I'm going to write until the book's out,' I cautioned.

'Why, are we hiding anything?'

'No.'

'So I will read it' – he mimics the act of reading a book intently – 'and then I will be happy, or not.'

'I think you will be mostly happy,' I told him. 'But one thing I want to reflect is the chaos. Because it says something about Albania, and what happens when a foreigner comes, and how that encounter works.' I tried, driving the fingers of one hand into the palm of the other, to indicate how the cultural exchange involved a kind of collision.

Ilir nodded. He got me, more or less.

'Consider it like home.'

The day of my departure was a sunny Sunday. I did a final breakfast shift, filling the garden with classical music amid questions and objections from all around me.

By the afternoon, it was raining again. Ilir counselled against calling a taxi – 'everyone will take one, because of the rain' – and refused to take payment for my bar bill. Then he came to the metal gates to see me off.

The distance to my new lodgings in Blloku was not great and my suitcase easy to trundle; soon enough I was in the right area. But I could not find the street where my host was waiting for me outside the house. I wandered awhile, hoping that each turning would be the right one. Then my phone rang; my host was wondering where I was. He attempted to direct me to where I would find him – 'an old man with a red umbrella' – but between his broken English and my inability to read my surroundings, I was not much the wiser. I wandered some more. My host rang again and this time, I collared a passing young man and handed him the phone. Successful communication took place and soon I found myself in a street lined with Italian villas where an old man with a red umbrella was waiting for me.

My accommodation was a self-contained flat adjoining the house in which my host and his wife had lived for decades. As he showed me around, Aleksander tried to convey the essence of Albania to me. 'Our flag – red and black. The red is blood, and the black is death. I tell you this because you are a WRITER.' His sentence ended with the emphatic inflection I had come to recognise as characteristic of the way some people spoke when communicating something important. Albanian was the root for other languages, he went on: the first words people in the region had used for aspects of their environment, such as field and river, had been in Albanian. 'Do you know the word for mountain?' he asked. 'Mons' – the root is Albanian.'

Alexander, the name he and I almost shared, denoted someone who was 'born in the dream', while Cassandra meant 'one who dreams'. Given the limits of his English, it was hard to know exactly what he meant, but it seemed he was suggesting that Albanian was a kind of ur-language through which the first humans of south eastern Europe had named their world into being. I loved the idea and let the images of a wonder-struck humanity naming their world into being float over me.

I was pleased with my new accommodation. The flat was composed of a decent-sized living room with a large corner sofa and TV and a kitchenette that faced the street. There was a generous bathroom with a shower, bath and washing machine. The bedroom was at the back, an oasis of white with French windows that opened onto a small balcony looking onto a walled garden. Behind it rose the gracious form of another Italian villa.

It was all so soothing to the eye and spirit. Or would have been, for as soon as I raised my eyes a little higher where the sky should have been loomed a tower composed of red and blue panels.

The next morning I awoke to the thud of powerful machinery pounding the earth and the clang of metal against metal. I lay in the white bed and thought of the morning sounds of the hostel: the chopping of the break-fast veg, the bubble of familiar voices and the wail of the nearby mosques. BASH BOOM! BASH!

The sounds of construction continued throughout the day as I came and went, exploring my new area. My new neighbourhood lacked the down-to-earthness of Kavaja Street. Instead of delicatessens, market stalls and bakeries were banks, restaurants and pharmacies and it was harder to find fresh food. This was the working part of Tirana, the place where people came to do business or to meet, in a see-and-be-seen kind of way, in the trendy bars and cafes. The pavements were full of professional-looking people walking purposefully up and down. Even the smells were different, with perfumes and aftershaves wafting over the car fumes.

In Hoxha's time, Blloku had been the enclave where the dictator and his politburo spent most of their lives. It was both a prison and a place of immense privilege: 'Blloku i Udhëheqësve', the Leaders' Block, was guarded by soldiers and plain-clothes secret police. It had special shops which stocked Western clothes and groceries unavailable to the general population. Its inhabitants' homes were staffed by housekeepers and servants. But their personal lives were severely curtailed: the Blloku elite married amongst themselves, maintaining a tight network of political alliances that helped to keep them in power.

My visiting friend had a connection with the trip on which I had not visited Albania all those years ago: my tour of the Eastern Bloc had ended in Istanbul where she had lived for a year. Thirty years later, she arrived in Tirana just before Easter. 'Mmm.' She sniffed the air appreciatively as we took our first stroll around the streets. 'Reminds me a bit of Istanbul. I could live here. They like their pop music, don't they?'

We sampled the amenities of the post-communist Block with a celebratory meal. The restaurant was a little pricey even for us; there was no way ordinary locals could afford to eat there. We drank raki in Kometiti and made pretend calls on the rotary phones. We scaled the Pyramid as far as we dared and, relaxing at the flat, watched Edvin read the news on TV.

Then we embarked on a serious programme of communist sightseeing. I had saved some of Tirana's most important sights for her visit, notably the vast underground bunker the Hoxha regime had built in case of nuclear attack. Bunkers were an Albanian speciality. Between 1967 and 1986, the government had carried out a policy of 'bunkerization', constructing concrete shelters across the land as refuges should the country be invaded by a foreign force. They dotted the country's towns and cities and guarded its borders and beaches, a physical manifestation of Hoxha's paranoia. The plan had been to for 700,000 bunkers, but only around 170,000 were built in the end. In any case, with each one reportedly costing the price of a two-bedroom apartment, the bunkers made a significant contribution to the impoverishment of the country.

I had barely registered their presence in Tirana. With their the squat domes and slits like mechanical mouths, the bunkers vaguely reminded me of the daleks in Doctor Who. But they seemed largely irrelevant; as a city-dweller, I was used to disregarding the infrastructure of the past.

But the bunkers above Tirana were hard to ignore. We had taken the fifteen-minute cable car ride up Mount Dajti, an excursion some 1600 meters above sea level popular with both tourists and locals. As the cable car processed skywards, the towers and apartment blocks disappeared and the city became a modest settlement set in a lush green landscape. At the summit we rejoiced in the freshness of the air and the beauty of the hillside. Spring flowers sprung out of the woodland floor and wild ponies grazed among the trees. But exploring this new paradise, we soon noticed the domes watching us. 'They're like eyes,' said my friend. 'It's really quite ominous.'

Another morning, we took a bus to the city outskirts to visit Bunk'Art. This was a bunker on a grand scale: five floors with a hundred and six rooms and an assembly hall carved into the mountain. There, Hoxha and his politburo would live and plan while Albania was under attack. The attack never happened and, post-communism, the facility had been converted into a museum with a trendy name and a colourful logo. We bought our tickets, eyed the merchandise in the Bunk Shop and headed towards the door in the mountainside.

The passage was narrow and a notice instructing us not to panic should the museum's electricity generator fail gave me pause. I did not like enclosed, windowless spaces. Pressing on, we went through a series of heavy concrete doors with huge metal handles. Combined with a shower in the decontamination room, it was hoped they would protect the politburo from the ill effects of radiation.

And there we were, in the private quarters of the dictator himself. On the counter in the lobby sat a large black phone; a sign invited visitors to listen to a recording of Hoxha's voice. Picking up the receiver, my friend enacted an imagined conversation with him about me: 'No, I'm not telling you her name'. The other party must have been persuasive because before she'd replaced the receiver she'd told him my first name and lied about my age.

The armchairs in the little sitting room next door were so inviting that we sat down. On the coffee table between them was a glass ashtray and a plastic photo album of the kind popular in the 1960s. I leafed through it but soon put it back down. The black and white pictures took me straight into a world that seemed rather personal. Could the photos be real? Instead of feeling pleased at having a level of access unthinkable in a Western tourist attraction, an uncomfortable feeling rose in me: *I don't like it, this proximity to this man and the things of his world.*

We were surprised by modesty of the dictator's bedroom: it was just big enough for a double bed with a red satin bedspread and a nightstand set against the re-enforced wall. Then, following some more passages through the mountain, we arrived at the auditorium. This was more like it, a large chamber with rows of red velvet seats in front of a nice little stage. You could imagine the entire politburo there, perhaps watching some footage of enemy action or holding presentations to discuss military strategy. 'STOP SMOKING' instructed a sign on the wall.

The social history section of the museum was also easier to take. There was a school room with bottles of ink on the low wooden desks and a shop selling jams and other food stuffs by weight. In the reconstructed living room of a typical Albanian home hung a paper calendar for 1973. Wooden cabinets recalled the dark furniture I'd known in the homes of old people while growing up. And yet they looked older, simpler: all the country's furniture was produced in state-owned wood factories to the same design, differing only in finish and size. The kinship between the sofa and chairs upholstered in a beige floral pattern and the communist sofa at the hostel was plain. In the dining room next door, the four empty dishes and water jug set out on the little table screamed scarcity. The metal stove which bore the single pot of food looked flimsy, as if it had come out of a doll's house.

In the House of Leaves, we again resorted briefly to the defence mechanism of levity, my friend enacting a mock interrogation about my life in Tirana. The red brick villa in the city centre was so-called because of the ivy that crawled up its walls and over the metal bars on its windows. As the headquarters of the notorious National Intelligence Service, it was also known as the House of Spies. For 46 years, the Sigurumi were 'the eyes and ears of the regime', drawing on a force of volunteers to surveil and inform on their fellow citizens. It was not clear how many people were involved: figures published by the

Ministry of the Interior put the figure at 200,000 but according to some estimates, one in every three or four people had acted as informants. The information-gathering operation was extensive: by 1990, the Sigurimi had around a million files, one for every adult member of the population. They contained details about their relationships and sexual preferences as well as their political views. The novelist Kadare's file ran to 1280 pages in four volumes. Recent years had seen repeated calls for the files to be made available to the public amid fears that people in prominent positions had something to hide.

The museum had remained virtually intact and its glass cases contained much of the original surveillance equipment. The secret police had used a vast array of cameras and recording devices and placed a great emphasis on tapping and bugging. The regime had invested in the best equipment available, making arrangements with more advanced countries to train staff in surveillance techniques. But it was hard, from the perspective of the twenty-first century, to imagine how much damage such tiny, outdated devices could do to the psyche of a nation. Looking into the display cabinets, I recognised some binoculars like my father's and dictaphones resembling the Walkmans of the 1980s. There was a camera from Germany. Despite all its claims to self-sufficiency, communist Albania had needed to import the technology of surveillance from abroad.

Outside, a young guide waved us towards an opening in the ground. The tunnel ran under the house and was part of a network of 12000 tunnels under the city – would we like to see it? We descended briefly into the earth, returning quickly to the surface out of respect for my claustrophobia.

'The tunnels were mainly to create a sense of the enemy,' the young man told us. 'They would even let off sirens to make you think of the danger.'

'Who was the enemy?' asked my friend.

'Everybody was the enemy and no one was the enemy.'

The first targets were the rich: his grandparents were imprisoned early in the regime because his grandmother descended from wealthy stock. Later, communism brought great poverty. His grandmother would make this much coffee – he indicated an amount little more than a centimetre – in a cup and allow members of the family to smell it. Coffee for drinking had to be saved for guests.

'Albania still has a communist mentality,' he went on. 'People today are paying the consequences. Some people are saying the files should be opened up and made public, but it wouldn't help Albania.'

Marinel had been given a volunteer role because the museum had no French-speaking attendant. Since he was trilingual with a Masters in cultural studies, we wondered why he didn't have a paid position. 'You have to pay to get a job, or have a friend,' he explained. 'The two guides employed here are friends with the manager.'

It could be stressful working at the museum, he went on, because some of the older Albanians found the exhibits traumatising. Seeing the interrogation chair, one woman had burst into tears. The young generation, meanwhile, didn't seem to care.

We had just seen evidence of this. In an upstairs room of the museum, a smartly-dressed old man was finishing a talk to a group of high school students. As a former political prisoner, he had a lot to tell the new generation about their country's recent past. But as they filed out of the room his young audience seemed nonchalant and nonplussed. Their evident disconnection from what they'd just heard made me feel frustrated for the speaker as I watched him walking down the corridor.

'Go after him,' urged my friend. 'Get his number.'

A few days later I meet Uran in a cafe filled with pop music. He is dressed with the same formality as before, in a black suit and shirt topped with a black trilby, and his manner is courtesy itself. But a conversational double-bind soon emerges; as a former political prisoner, he feels both obliged to communicate his experiences to the wider world and finds it difficult to do so.

'I am not sure what you want from me, what you want to know,' he says.

'I would like to hear about your experiences under communism,' I tell him.

'It is not easy to explain to another person what happened.' He pulls a packet of cigarettes from his pocket, extracts a cigarette and lights it. 'First of all, I want to say to you that it was a terrible time.'

The waiter is hovering. Uran orders a coffee and I ask for a mint tea.

Gradually, I manage to piece together the details of his life. He had been sent to prison at the age of twenty-three for writing a poem critical of the regime. The arrest did not come as a surprise: his father had spent ten years in prison in the early years of the regime. Uran had understood its oppressive nature from the outset and had never had any illusions that those who engaged in free expression could expect better treatment.

'I stayed in the prison twenty years, from 1961 to 1981. After this time, they left me outside for one year only and they sent me to a remote, isolated place, and not to move from there until communism fell. After five years, I went outside, like other people.' He pauses. 'But I want to say one thing to you, Gentle Lady. All Albanian people were in prison, even outside.'

The arrival of my drink – a mint tea bag soaking in a glass of hot milk – momentarily distracts me. Deciding against sending it back, I press Uran to give me a sense of life in prison.

'It was hell,' he replies. 'I was in Burrel, a building with one floor of one hundred and twenty metres, ten rooms and twenty-five people in every room.' Individuals were repeatedly put into solitary confinement for a month at a time, he especially because of his tendency to be outspoken. 'The food was very bad. With that food we couldn't live, but fortunately our families sent us from outside. Some of us died inside in that place. When someone was sick, no one helped. Some of us remained alive; this was by the help of God.'

I ask whether his experience had made him despair of humanity. But he only hears the word 'despair'.

'Listen to me, Gentle Lady. I hated the regime so much that I didn't want to show them that I am despairing. I wanted to show the communists that I am strong, that I didn't care about them. Some other people – good people – didn't know very well what the communist regime was. They were weaker, because they waited to be liberated. They were good, not to make noise, to speak out against communist, to wait for liberation. I didn't wait!' The last phrase has an emphatic uplift.

Resting in the ashtray while he talks, his cigarette has burnt into a long column of ash. He lights another and repeats: 'Gentle Lady, communism is the most terrible thing in the world.'

'Twenty years is a very long time to be in prison,' I say. 'I can't imagine what you do with your mind.'

Uran nods. The hatred he felt for the regime fuelled him with a determination to survive while his passion for reading and writing gave him something to do. The gaolers were happy to allow the prisoners books because they didn't believe they would survive long. So Uran taught himself Italian language and read Dante: 'I can recite to you, until now, the first part of The Divine Comedy!' he tells me with pride. Thereafter, he spent his days translating and writing. 'So these things helped me to resist. And so I remained alive, and am here now, with you.'

'Do you remember the day you came out?'

'I remember.' He draws on his cigarette. 'I went outside in 1981, it was a terrible time. You have to know something, Gentle Lady, that when I went outside I was in the prison more than inside the prison, because I couldn't speak any more like I did inside. In prison we spoke like in Parliament, but outside it was not possible because I have a younger brother. He told me the first day I was outside: "Uran, close the mouth. Don't speak out again because we are all in danger." I was compelled not to speak, and not speaking I was in prison!

'In 1991, communism fell, and I felt very well – I felt free.' He was given a job teaching Italian in a high school in Elbasan and elected head of the local Democratic Party. Two years later, he went to America to join his two nieces. But after a few years, he returned to Albania to spend his retirement writing poetry. 'The readers are here; no one understands me over there.'

'Now the political situation is not good. But what to do? Anyway, I am not in the prison any more. I am outside. I am talking with an English lady, I can write, I am good. I am good.' He lights another cigarette to replace the one that has burnt out in the ashtray and adds: 'To tell you the truth, not very good. I cannot change the situation!'

A life curtailed. By the time he was free he was approaching fifty and the chance to marry had passed.

'Did you go through a phase of being angry because they took twenty-five years of your life?'

'You have to know something,' he replies emphatically. 'I left my hate. People like me cannot hate profoundly, because I am a poet. They are bad people, they are not on a level with me. It is not important to speak about them individually, but I want to speak about the regime, about communist doctrine and to say to you and other people what a terrible thing communism is. This is my duty.'

'The rulers of the regime were ...' he searches for the words ... 'ignorant people. They had the power to do what they wanted but they are not lucky. I am lucky, because I didn't do anything bad to someone. They did bad to me! They should despair, not me.'

'Do you think there are communists left in Albania today?'

'Too many people!' he replies immediately. 'They are richer than me, they are stronger than me, and they are arrogant. I have nothing; they have too much. This regime now is like a communist regime. But no one puts me in the prison again, no one forbids me to speak with an English lady, no one stops me writing.'

He repeats: 'And now I am speaking with a gentle lady, it is good!'

Every day, he reads in Italian and Albanian and does some writing, often Albanian sonnets using the Petrarchan form. 'You may be surprised, but now I begin to read Shakespeare – Macbeth.'

We evoke, with mutual pleasure, the dagger scene and Macbeth's courage when fighting Macduff in the knowledge that he will die. 'The monologue "Tomorrow and tomorrow" I like very much,' muses Uran. 'And Iago in Othello – an interesting character.'

And then suddenly, as if remembering something, he is saying his goodbyes and leaving.

Watching his departing back for the second time, I feel sad. If I had been staying in Tirana longer, I could have visited him, given him the company of an English lady with a degree in literature. We could have read some Shakespeare together.

$$\mathscr{R} \quad 9 \quad \mathscr{R}$$

It was Easter Sunday and a beautiful day. I dragged my friend to church, twice. First we went to the Catholic one. Saint Paul's Cathedral was in the centre of Tirana, a modern construction built after the fall of communism with an undulating facade of coffee and cream. The stone form of Mother Teresa sat in prayer outside. Inside, the curling walls held people of all ages; the church was full and even the upper balconies had congregation. The service began with a procession of clergy like those I'd seen in Anglican churches and featured hymns I recognised from my Church of England upbringing. The only perceptible difference came from the people standing in the aisle filming the proceedings. Otherwise, the ecclesiastical sights and sounds were all-too-familiar. Soon we slipped away.

The evening service at the Orthodox church, by contrast, had all the opacity an amateur anthropologist could desire. The Resurrection of Christ Orthodox Cathedral was another mark of the return of religion to Albania. Completed in 2012 on the site of the cathedral destroyed by the regime, it was a modern take on the Byzantine, a dome on a substantial square with doors of gold. Its interior was a world of eastern glory, light filtering down through an arcade of windows. We took our seats facing an iconostasis of icons set in white marble.

But the focus of the service was sound. To the left of the iconostasis, around twenty men in scarlet robes stood in a circle, their backs to the congregation. At first they talked, as if amongst themselves, in a language of ritual that was impenetrable to me. After a time, they began to chant, the male voices weaving a polyphonic harmony with an undertow of deep base. As the ritual progressed, the congregation became more involved, standing and sitting at points that we couldn't predict. We joined the collective movement as best we could and at one point were reprimanded by a woman behind for crossing our legs. Time flowed on. The thought that the service would end became a distant one and the idea of leaving before it did impossible. I could feel the chanting working through and in my body. I was enclosed by a wall of sound.

And then the congregation was kissing the floor, some people going up to the chancel to kiss the figure of Christ. The service was ending. When we finally found ourselves outside, we saw that we had been in the church for an hour and a half. I felt all the better for it.

'Enver Hoxha's fight against religion was a campaign of unprecedented cruelty and one of the saddest chapters of his regime,' writes his biographer Blendi Fevzi. For Hoxha, a man who wanted to define meaning and purpose for an entire population, religion perhaps represented the ultimate rival. 'The only religion of Albania is Albanianisn,' he wrote, citing a line from the nineteenth-century poem *O moj Shqiperi* ('O Albania') by Pashdo Vasa. At the same time, he recognised the importance of faith to Albanians, instructing local branches of the party 'to be cautious, but ruthless' in their attempts to eradicate religion as it was 'still very influential among the people'.

When the Communists took power in 1944, about seventy per cent of Albania's population was Muslim, with most of the remaining thirty per cent Orthodox or Catholic Christians. Around seventeen per cent or 200,000 people were Bektashis, a Sufi mystical sect originating in Asia.

The persecution of Catholics, with their international ties and respect for the authority of the Vatican, began early on. The Jesuit and Franciscan orders based in the country were told to terminate their missionary activities and Catholic institutions were forbidden from having anything to do with the education of the young.

In February 1967, Hoxha gave a speech which officially launched the battle against 'religious ideology'. Religion was 'the opium of the people' and those who were 'poisoned' by it must be 'cured'. By the end of that year, decree no. 4,337 banned the practising of all religions. All remaining places of worship were closed down, their assets confiscated by the state. Churches, mosques and other religious buildings were demolished or turned into bars and restaurants, cultural centres and youth clubs. The Cathedral of Shkoder became an indoor sports arena and the Heart of Christ Church in Tirana a cinema. Bonfires were made of religious books and artefacts. Young people and students, conscripted by the regime, carried out much of the work. Muslim and Christian believers were denigrated as 'backward' or traitors who worked with Western powers.

Nine years later, religious belief was outlawed and Albania became the world's first and only atheist country. Article 37 of the constitution declared: 'The State recognises no religion, and supports atheistic propaganda in order to implant a scientific materialistic world outlook in the people'. The penal code introduced the following year imposed prison sentences of three to ten years for 'religious propaganda and the production, distribution, or storage of religious literature.'

Over the decades, thousands of imams and priests were imprisoned, forced into hard labour or executed. The Bektashis had it bad: in 1947, amid growing persecution, the Bektashi leader was coerced into shooting two imams and subsequently killed himself. In an vindictive violation of the religious prohibition on shaving, Bektashi imams had their beards shaved off in public. The regime said beards were 'unhygienic'.

The irony – was it also part of the reason? – was that Hoxha's family had in all likelihood been Bektashi. The name Hoxha meant 'imam'.

Having investigated minority sects such as the Druze in Lebanon and the Sufis in Britain, I was keen to learn more about Bektashism. The Bektashi faith, which incorporated some of the beliefs of Shia Islam and Christian practices, seemed to be another instantiation of a tolerant, universalist spirituality that avoided the dogmatism of mainstream religion. Historically such spiritual freethinkers tended to have a hard time with the authorities. The Bektashi were banned from Turkey, where they had their world headquarters, under Ataturk's secular rule. In 1925 they transferred the headquarters to Tirana, building a centre that was completed in 1941 but closed under Hoxha in 1967. The Bektashi World Centre reopened in 1991 and been restored with the help of various grants. Under Albanian law, Bektashis now had full legal status as a separate religion with their own national holidays.

I emailed the head quarters requesting an interview and in due course was granted a Saturday morning appointment with Baba Mondi, the eighth spiritual leader of the sect.

The centre was situated in a hilltop garden to the east of Tirana. Arriving early, we wandered around the site, trying to take in the set-up. It was not like any religious complex I had ever seen: it was neither a church nor monastery, mosque nor meeting hall. The central building – a tekke or temple – was an elaborate domed structure encircled by ornate arches. But while the tekke was for the Bektashi to gather, it was not exclusively for the purpose of worship. It was open to all: the kind of etiquette for entering the religious space of another group such as the removing of shoes or donning of headscarves was not required.

We wandered around the centre's museum, only half-understanding what we saw. There was a life-sized model of a former dede, clad in white robes and a long jacket of green, a sacred colour for the Bektashi. Glass cases contained seals, rosaries and earrings, pendants and rings worn by former dede. Jewellery was clearly an important part of the clerical dress.

My correspondent in arranging the interview had described herself as lawyer and chief of protocol. In person, Shelda was a handsome, self-possessed woman in her thirties. She showed us around, offering pieces of information she thought might be of interest. Men and women were not segregated as in conventional Islam, she told us, nor was there an obligation to pray – you prayed when you felt like it. The interior of the main hall was impressive, with floor-to-ceiling windows and columns of marble, its surfaces adorned with geometric and mandala-like designs in deep blues and mint greens. Shelda herself had got married there, in the 'celebration room'.

It was time for the interview. Shelda led me into a meeting room where the dede was waiting. He was attired like the model of his predecessor in white robes and a green jacket with matching cummerbund and turban. Edmond Brahimaj had been chosen as the Bektashi's eighth leader by a council of babas (fathers) in an election in 2011. 'Dede' – literally 'above the baba' – was a title that acknowledged the ancestral element of succession and the grandfatherly nature of the role.

I set my laptop down down on the table, noticing the bowls of sweets which, according to custom in the Middle East, enabled the host to send visitors away with something sweet. I gained permission to record and the interview began, with Shelda translating my questions and the dede's answers.

The Bektashi were part of Shia Islam, he explained, and believed in the twelve imams. But they respected all faiths and considered the afterlife open to all. 'All for us are brother and sister,' he said; the important thing was our shared humanity.

Under communism, many Bektashi properties had been confiscated and many imams killed, he went on. The Bektashi continued to worship in secret, pretending to celebrate the birthday of a family member when they were in fact marking a religious holiday. The sect had been rebuilding the religion since the 1990s. The buildings were the easier part: people were more difficult and there were not many imams. It was hard to know how many Bektashis there were in Albania now, since the government census did not show the true figures. The Bektashi had contributed a lot to Albania including Skanderbeg and some famous writers. The current President of Albania was Bektashi.

Interviewing a religious leader was always a formal affair; that I well knew. But my polite questions were yielding very standard answers and I felt we were going through the motions. Evidently the dede did too, as he frequently checked the smartphone on the table beside him.

I tried to switch the focus to more pressing concerns. 'What can the Bektashi do to help Albania at this difficult time?'

'We don't speak in a political way but in a human way,' came the reply. The Bektashi worked with poor people and tried to persuade young Albanians to stay and improve their country rather than emigrate.

A last question about his experience of leadership elicited a surprising response. His mother had fertility problems and when she was pregnant with him, the doctors had predicted he would be stillborn. 'But I lived and I also have three other brothers and sisters!' He attributed the miracle to the previous Bektashi leader who had prayed that his mother would be fertile, telling her: 'I will give these children to you, and to me also.' And so it was that Edmond grew up steadfast in faith and, when communism fell, entered the priesthood. It was important, he added, to recognise that his leadership was not the result of his personal qualities: 'This wasn't my capability, it was from God'.

I turned off the recording, thanked him and prepared to leave. But the dede seemed to want to talk some more.

'May God complete your desires,' he said. There was something about the deliberate way he said it that made me respond openly.

'I have too many,' I told him.

'God completes something other than what you want,' he consoled. 'God gives difficulties to those he wants. The bad things are easy to get; good things take time.'

Now we were talking. This was spiritual advice, straight from him to me. 'God is where you are not looking,' he added.

'I will remember that,' I promised.

He took a fistful of sweets from the bowl on the table and pressed them into my hand. Then another: 'And that is for your friend.'

In the lobby we posed for photos, the dede's arm around my shoulder. As we gathered our things to leave, he was already greeting some visiting children, dispensing sweets to them in a grandfatherly way.

❧ 10 ❧

The garden behind the villa was in leaf, its collection of low trees resembling a little orchard. Some roses were already in bloom, their pink flowers bright against the fresh green. But the spring growth didn't block out the harsh lines of the new stadium and the tower looming above. The sight made me sad: the transformation of the city into blocks of high-rise concrete threatened to erase much of Tirana's charm.

'Of course there'll still be grass left: they can't take it all. A few thin slices of field in the gaps between houses like green fish fingers, and maybe some wistful trees craning for a view of the undeveloped sky still wild with black-birds and rooks.' [1]

I read the poetic tweet the day I discovered that the construction noises came from the Vertical Forest Tower being built behind the stadium. Its poignancy captured my mood as I researched Tirana's development plans. The tower would have twenty-one floors and, according to the architectural blurb, feature green facades that would 'open like a flower' with thousands of bushes, shrubs and trees.

Reading this, I was baffled. Even maintaining my small, semi-wild garden in England required consistent effort and this was a city that lacked basic infrastructure. Dumpsters on every street took the place of house-to-house waste collection and there were no recycling facilities. Many of the rooftops bore water tanks because, despite a wealth of spring water from the mountains, the city did not have reliable running water. How would the blooming tower be maintained? And even if it were, wouldn't it be at odds with the rest of Tirana?

The explanation for the Forest Tower lay in political ambition. A masterplan to transform the city centre had been published in 2016 under the name Tirana 2030. The idea was to re-create the centre of the city as a place of high-density dwellings and tourist facilities. There would be more bike lanes and green spaces; car use would be discouraged. The origins of the plan went back to 2003 when, as mayor, Rama had designed a masterplan in which the construction of towers was central: Skanderbeg Square would be surrounded by ten tall towers, with more towers flanking The Boulevard. A few years later, a masterplan for an 'urban neighbourhood' on the edge of the Artificial Lake included the construction of … towers.

The new approach to urban development stood in stark opposition to what had gone below, with the low Ottoman houses and Italian villas. Even when large apartment blocks were constructed under Hoxha, the height of the buildings was limited to five floors. No wonder Tirana's new towers were such an interruption of the skyline.

As mayor, Rama had gleaned international plaudits for rescuing the city from Soviet gloom. Announcing him as the winner of the inaugural World Mayor Prize in 2004, the award committee said: 'Edi Rama is the man who changed a whole city. Now there is a new Tirana, colored, happy, with a new and improved infrastructure and cultural life.' But while painting existing buildings was relatively cheap, transforming Tirana into a city of towers was expensive. By the time Rama became Prime Minister of Albania in 2013, only a few had been built.

His successor as mayor, also a member of the Socialist Party, embraced the masterplan with enthusiasm. Instead of keeping an election promise to put a moratorium on building permits, Veliaj had approved the building of the 24-storey Eyes of Tirana and nearby Book Building in Skanderbeg Square.

It was high time I learnt more about the dynamics at play in Tirana's changing physical fabric. But who from? An architecture academic would be ideal. In a country so fraught with vested interests, would it be possible to find an expert with a degree of detachment? Looking online at the profiles of various academics, one stood out. There was something about the way Saimir Kristo at Polis University presented himself that suggested a critical intelligence able to survive the high politics and trendy jargon of Tirana's architectural scene.

I meet Saimir at the Radio Bar in Blloku. The place is retro-communism on steroids, a medley of turquoise, red and yellow, its walls crammed with pictures and vintage radios and the air is full of jazzy music and lively chatter. Saimir is at a table, waiting. He is perhaps in his late thirties and has a definite spark about him.

'I've heard a lot about towers,' I say by way of opening gambit.

'What have you heard about our towers?' The response comes with something between a flash and a twinkle. He's giving nothing away.

'That they have been built very fast,' I say carefully.

This time, the response is even less direct. 'Let's see,' he says. 'I can give you a general overview of Tirana. I can even make you a sketch, if you want. I can make it in the phone, or the notebook.'

I hand him my notebook and he's off, sketching and talking. Tirana was never founded properly, beginning more or less spontaneously as a trading post for passing caravans. A mosque was built, followed by a hammam and a bakery and, before long, mosques and bakeries were popping up everywhere. 'And this was Tirana, up to 1912.'

I watch as he builds the drawing carefully; it's clear he loves teaching. I know some of what he's telling me, but it is nice having my own personal tutor who can cut through all the detail and give me the key points.

'Only a hundred years ago?' I ask.

'Yes, a village. Twenty thousand people. Nothing on the east side of the river, nothing.'

Albania's short-lived period of independence was followed by the first world war and attempts from surrounding powers to take over the country. The construction of its administrative centre was the fruit of King Zog's alliance with Mussolini.

'Zog let the fascists take over the city,' Saimir explains. The king had wanted to show he could recreate Albania in the image of Italy, so he brought in the best architects from Florence. 'Here they would mark a boulevard, and they would use this axis from north to south and the river for west to east.'

'Of course, in 1945 you have the dictator.' His pen is still working. 'He had The Boulevard as the souvenir of the Italians and houses as the legacy of the Ottomans. Then he built these big blocks, communist blocks.' It was an attempt by the latest ruler to remake the city according to his vision.

'So each regime is expressing its power through architecture?'

'Yes, exactly.'

'Why? Cities don't normally develop like that.'

Saimir nods. 'Let me go through the last stage.' The fall of communism led to an explosion of construction. Suddenly it was possible to do business in Tirana while the collapse of state-provided services in rural areas drew large numbers of people to the city. There was a huge need for more housing and other buildings. Without planning or regulation, people built everywhere, including on the eastern side of the river. Then along came Rama with A Plan that promised to put an end to the chaos and created the first framework for the towers. Then came another mayor and another plan – 'New towers here, new towers here, new towers here, new towers here – I'm not drawing for fun,' Saimir assures me. 'I know what I'm doing … new towers *here*.'

He stops drawing and we look at the sketch. Part of the justification for building so many towers was tourism, he explains, since each tower is to contain a hotel. 'The idea is that you promote a city, you make it a trend city, then you say you need more hotels in the city centre because that's where the demand is, and then you build the towers.' But, with Albanians queuing up to emigrate, the plan doesn't make sense. Who will buy all the new flats?

Saimir's mini-lesson confirms my impression there's something fundamentally abnormal about the mishmash that is the Albanian capital. In contrast to cities which have developed organically or according to a coherent plan, its jumble of buildings and spaces tell the story of a power struggle. Or rather, a series of power struggles: every regime tried to erase the memory of the previous order and replace it with its own version. The latest attempt to turn Tirana into a city of towers is no different.

I understand what he's saying, I tell him, but I'm not sure what he *thinks*.

'Ah, what I *think*.' The tone is lightly ironic. 'The historic core is being lost ... if you destroy the Ottoman buildings and Italian period houses, then Tirana is a tabula rasa. I believe in the preservation of cultural heritage, the preservation of monuments and the memory of the city and this is being lost.'

Far from creating a green city, the level of construction in Tirana is causing pollution, he goes on. The politicians' plans do not contain green spaces of any size, while many former parks are being destroyed for the new buildings. The planning rules do little to stop big companies to building profitable real estate. 'It's something you don't really need to investigate a lot. Just take a walk around the city. It's obvious!'

'There are many historical buildings from the Ottoman period or the Italian period and many others are being destroyed in the name of profits. For example, you already have the stadium which is demolished, and you have a new stadium – a bizarre situation – we have a stadium and a tower! You cannot bring the stadium in the city centre when you haven't solved the transport problem. Imagine that neighbourhood when there's a game; you will paralyse the whole city!'

'And this forest tower … ' I begin.

He shoots me a look sparkling with irony. 'Oh, come on. Come *on.*'

There's a silence in which we allow the ridiculous notion of a tower of plants to settle.

'Look, there are towers of the same design in Milan or China but they require a huge amount of maintenance costs,' he continues. 'Tirana is not this kind of city. I worry about the future of this city after all this speculative construction. You need a more natural development; you are imposing a new structure which citizens are not ready to accept.'

'I haven't met anyone so far who likes what's happening,' I say.

He nods. Living conditions in the city were contributing to Albania's brain drain. 'We should be very worried about the low number of births and the big number of people who want to leave – people who have several masters,

PhDs, are experts in their field. But the people don't want to live in the stress of Tirana.'

The development of public space is essentially a political matter, he goes on, one that requires a high level of engagement from the public. 'Politics requires a maturity from the people: if the maturity doesn't arrive, everything is lost. I believe the new generation of Albanians need to be more active, to speak up. They have to be really responsible citizens; it's not about one or two, it's about 500 000, one million people.'

'Are they architecturally literate?' I think of the political maturity demonstrated by the students and wonder how far that extends to an understanding of public space.

'I think it will take some time for people to be more aware of the importance of not only private property, but public property, of the common good,' he replies. 'If you think about the trends globally – that public land should be privatised – we are talking about the opposite. Space is a public good; it should not be left to someone private. The public consciousness of public space is still not cultivated; this is our job. You said yourself that no one you've met so far in Tirana likes what is happening – this is it!'

Our talk is coming to a natural end. But before we part, I want his take on the impact of Tirana's mountainous surroundings on life in the city.

'I love mountains!' He laughs happily at the mere thought of them. 'Albania is a country of big geographical contrasts – all the Balkans are the same – it's a beautiful thing. In Tirana, we have already lost the relationship the mountain had with the buildings of the city. One of the principles that was used in the past is that buildings would be no more than five storeys high, so that from every window you would see the mountain.'

If you kept in mind where the mountain was and built east-west, you would always have natural light and, looking out of the window, see where the sun was on the mountain. In a hundred years of change, the mountain had been the one constant element of Tirana.

'That's magical,' I say.

'Yes,' he agrees. 'It's magical. But unfortunately we've lost it!'

A couple of nights before I was due to fly home, I paid a final visit to the hostel. Ilir had gone south and the two longterm volunteers were leaving, at least for a time. Apart from the permanent staff, the temporary community was dissolving. I had tried and failed, twice more, to get the words of 'The Pick and Gun'. It was as if the window that had opened up onto the past had shut again.

The day of my flight coincided with a protest which would block the main road to the airport. Aleks booked me a taxi with plenty of time ahead, instructing the driver to take the back roads. Then I sat down with him and his wife Dhuata for tea. With my visiting friend and glut of inter-views, I'd been too busy to make the most of the couple's openness. But my last two hours in Tirana accidentally brought a chance to talk to members of the older genera-tion about about how their city had changed.

'Tirana was very different now from when we were young,' began Aleks. 'It was a much smaller city, of perhaps around 30000 people, during the communist era. When I was little, my street was the new bazaar area – the street with the stores. There were only small buildings and a lot of dirt around them.'

'A house had a big garden, with flowers, and one or two storeys the maximum,' added Dhuata.

'There were no personal cars,' said Aleks. 'When you entered the yard there were two lines of flowers and pomegranates. We got water from the well. Life was safe. We could walk by ourselves to school. Sometimes the nurse came to check for lice. Every morning we put our hands out for the teacher to see if our nails were clean.

'She checked if you'd changed your underwear!' laughed Dhuata.

'We played hide and seek until it got dark – hopscotch, piggy back, chess,' recalled her husband. 'We knew everybody, almost everybody.'

'Now it's more free, said Dhuata. 'The mentality has changed, it's like in Europe, where people live together before getting married.'

The couple's description vividly evoked the old life and the beauty that coexisted with its limitations. What I couldn't see was how it had disappeared almost entirely in such a short space of time.

'Tell me how it got from that to this and what's happening now,' I said.

'It started with democracy,' replied Aleks. 'Everybody started to build where he wanted to build.' He added with emphasis: '*You could build wherever wanted to build.*'

'In the parks, everywhere,' supplied Dhuata.

Aleks nodded. 'The parks were full of buildings. The river was built on so much you could not see the water. You could find a building that was seven storeys high: all the dirt from these buildings made a bad smell. Most of The Boulevard was full of buildings: cafes, restaurants.'

'It looked more like a city from Afghanistan than Europe!' said Dhuata.

'You could not see the mountain when you came from the airport because of the dust from the building work,' continued Aleks. 'The road was full of holes and dirt; you could not drive more than in first gear. Edi Rama transformed all this; that is why I wrote the book.'

He picked up a book from the table and handed it to me. The cover displayed a younger version of Rama standing against a blue sky. The author was Aleks himself.

'He threw down all the buildings and cleared everything,' he said approvingly.

'He stood up to the people, the mafia who built all these buildings,' agreed Dhuata.

'As prime minister, he transformed the city of Tirana,' said Aleks. 'He cleared the park at Rinia and made the big park. He planted a lot of trees. He started the colours with the government buildings.'

'Even the mayor is very good,' added Dhuata.

I was puzzled. The couple seemed pleased with the very

politicians who were destroying their traditional neighbourhood. Out loud, I asked: 'What do you think of the masterplan and the towers?'

'We don't like them so much,' said Dhuata. 'It's not nice to live with all these big buildings.

'I think money is governing Albania, as is happening all over the world,' said Aleks. 'When I came to this street, there were only two-storey villas. Now we have a new law and they can build up to six storeys.'

'I grew up next door,' said Dhuata. 'The whole street had two floor villas with big gardens and flowers.'

'Why don't you protest?' I asked. Everyone else seemed to.

Dhuata shrugged. 'We are just a few people here. Who would hear us?'

'Do you like Albania?' asks the taxi driver. He's successfully avoided the roadblocks and I will be at the airport with plenty of time to spare. We are cruising along an open road in the hour before sunset. The landscape looks beautiful in the golden light.

I did, I told the driver truthfully. In terms of its stated objectives, Tirana hadn't made it, that was clear. Nothing was working well; basic infrastructure was lacking and the plans for the future unrealisable. Living standards were low and for most of its inhabitants, life was a struggle. The politics were dysfunctional and corruption ubiquitous. Attitudes towards women and the disabled were from a bygone age. And yet, and yet … there was something so alive about the place, a spirit that moved amongst the chaos. The longing of the Albanian people, after their decades cut off from the world, to be part of the West was endearing. Albania was a child of a country wanting to be seen, desperate for connection with the rest of us.

Yes, Tirana was a mess, but I loved it all the same.

BIBLIOGRAPHY

Fred C. Abrahams, *Modern Albania: From Dictatorship to Democracy in Europe*, New York University Press, 2015

Hannah Arendt, *The Origins of Totalitarianism*, Penguin Classics, 2017

Blendi Fevziu, *Enver Hoxha: The Iron Fist of Albania*, I.B. Tauris, 2016

NOTES

INTRODUCTION

1. Andrezj Stasiuk, *On the Road to Babadac: Travels in the Other Europe*, Vintage, 2012, p 93.

CHAPTER 10

1. Catherine Baker, Twitter, 10th April 2019.

ABOUT THE AUTHOR

Dr Alex Klaushofer is an author and journalist who has written extensively on social and affairs and politics in Britain and Middle East. Her work has appeared in publications such as *The Guardian* and *The Daily Telegraph*, along with contributions to BBC radio.

Her books combine reportage, travel writing and one or two other genres. *Paradise Divided* tells the human stories of modern-day Lebanon and explores the mix of social, religious and political forces that make up this complex country.

The Secret Life of God is a kind of spiritual investigation into twenty-first century Britain which chronicles how, in an ostensibly secular age, people are finding new ways of believing and belonging.

She writes essays about the changing times on Substack at Ways of Seeing: www.alexklaushofer.substack.com. Her website can be found at: www.alexklaushofer.com.